First Steps in ABAP®

Dr. Boris Rubarth

Dr. Boris Rubarth:
First Steps in ABAP®

ISBN: 978-1-4922-2787-8

Editor: Alice Adams

Cover Design: Philip Esch, Martin Munzel, Ulrike Peters

Cover Photo: fotolia

Interior Design: Johann-Christian Hanke

All rights reserved.

1st Edition 2013, Gleichen

© 2013 by Espresso Tutorials GmbH

URL: *www.espresso-tutorials.com*

All rights reserved. Neither this publication nor any part of it may be copied or reproduced in any form or by any means or translated into another language without the prior consent of Espresso Tutorials GmbH, Zum Gelenberg 11, 37130 Gleichen, Germany.

Espresso Tutorials makes no warranties or representations with respects to the content hereof and specifically disclaims any implied warranties of merchantability or fitness for any particular purpose. Espresso Tutorials assumes no responsibility for any errors that may appear in this publication.

Feedback
We greatly appreciate any kind of feedback you have concerning this book. Please mail us at *info@espresso-tutorials.com*.

Table of Contents

Preface		**5**
1	**Getting Started with ABAP**	**7**
	1.1 Hello ABAP	7
	1.2 Using the ABAP Editor	8
	1.3 Starting the report	13
	1.4 Using ABAP keyword documentation	15
	1.5 Viewing existing code	16
	1.6 Versioning your report	18
	1.7 Conclusion	18
2	**Using ABAP Statements**	**21**
	2.1 Using parameters as input variables	21
	2.2 Using conditional branches	25
	2.3 Using texts that can be translated	26
	2.4 Working with string variables	28
	2.5 Using elementary data types	30
	2.6 Debugging your report	33
	2.7 Conclusion	36
3	**Using the ABAP Workbench**	**37**
	3.1 Starting the ABAP Workbench	37
	3.2 Configuring ABAP Workbench options	39
	3.3 Working with packages and transport requests	41

	3.4 Transaction code for a report	46
4	**Using data types from ABAP Data Dictionary (DDIC)**	**51**
	4.1 Getting started with complex data types	51
	4.2 Working with the ABAP Data Dictionary (DDIC)	55
	4.3 Working with internal tables	60
5	**Modularization and reusing functionality**	**67**
	5.1 Using form routines	67
	5.2 Using function modules	71
	5.3 Using ABAP classes	90
	5.4 Exception concept for classes	101
6	**Accessing the database**	**105**
	6.1 Using ABAP statements to access the database	105
7	**ABAP User Interface Technologies**	**115**
	7.1 Working with messages	115
	7.2 Working with list processing	117
	7.3 Working with screens and DynPros	127
	7.4 Short overview on SAP UI technologies	144
8	**Conclusion**	**151**
A	**The Author**	**154**
B	**Disclaimer**	**155**

Preface

First Steps in ABAP offers an easy and straightforward path into the world of ABAP. It paves the way to your own ABAP code right from the start, always focuses on the rudiments you need to know for each step. The lessons build on each other, so you plan to read the book from start to finish in order to add on in each lesson. It is beneficial if you have knowledge of a development language. However this is not a strict prerequisite, you only have to be familiar with navigation in an ABAP system. After reading this introductory book, you will have an understanding of the foundation of ABAP and can decide which core area you would like to deepen your knowledge in.

We have added a few icons to our text that will help you access useful information. These include:

> **Tips**
>
> Tips highlight information concerning more details about the subject being described and/or additional background information.

> **Warnings**
>
> Warnings draw attention to information that you should be aware of when you go through the examples from this book on your own.

1 Getting Started with ABAP

Reports are a good starting point for familiarizing yourself with general ABAP principles and tools. Although modern user interface features aren't used, ABAP reports are still used in many areas.

This chapter will show how easy it is to write a simple *ABAP Report*. With the knowledge provided in this chapter, readers will be able to examine existing ABAP applications delivered by SAP or as part of a customer implementation project.

1.1 Hello ABAP

So let's get started with the common Hello World example:

```
WRITE 'Hello world!'.
```

Each ABAP statement starts with an *ABAP keyword* and ends with a period. Keywords must be separated by at least one *space*. It does not matter whether or not you use one or several lines for an ABAP statement.

Now where should you write this statement – in the text editor of your choice? No, you will need to enter your code using the *ABAP Editor*, which is part of ABAP Tools delivered with the *SAP NetWeaver Application Server ABAP* (AS ABAP). No ABAP code can be developed without AS ABAP – but you do not need access to a productive SAP system to start your work. The *SAP De-*

veloper Network (SDN) offers trial downloads that are a perfect starting point (*http://www.sdn.sap.com/irj/scn/nw-downloads*).

> **SAP NetWeaver Application Server ABAP (AS ABAP)**
>
> AS ABAP is an application server with its own database, ABAP runtime environment, and ABAP development tools (like the ABAP Editor). The AS ABAP offers a development platform (or virtual machine) that is independent of hardware, operating system, and database.

1.2 Using the ABAP Editor

Assuming that you are familiar with how to log on to and navigate in an SAP system, start transaction SE38 to navigate to the ABAP Editor.

The ABAP Editor is the tool used to view or to edit existing code, as well as create new code. Let's start creating a *Report*, which is one of several ABAP objects.

> **ABAP Reports**
>
> ABAP Reports were initially only used to "report" data (read data from the database), and are the easiest way to get started with ABAP. You can use reports to write data to the database as well. We will cover more on reports and other ABAP types later.

On the initial screen of the editor, specify the name of your report in the input field PROGRAM. Specify the name as ZHELLOWORLD01 as shown in Figure 1.1.

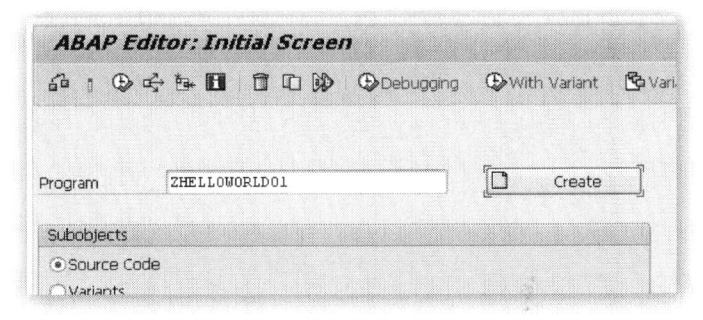

Figure 1.1: Initial screen of the ABAP Editor (transaction SE38)

The preceding Z is important for the name; the Z ensures that your report resides in the *Customer Namespace*.

You can type the report name in lower case letters, but the editor will change it to upper case – names of ABAP objects are not case sensitive.

> **Customer Namespace**
>
> The customer namespace includes all objects with the prefix Y or Z. It is always used when customers (or partners) create objects (like a report) to differentiate these objects from SAP's objects. This prevents name conflicts with objects that SAP delivers later. For example, SAP often delivers updated objects with Support Packages to provide corrections or legal updates to the system.

After specifying the name of the report, click the CREATE button. (The system will check that another report with that name does not exist.) A popup window ABAP: PROGRAM ATTRIBUTES will pop up and you will provide more information about your report.

First, you will have to provide a title for your report and then specify the report TYPE. For this example, we will select EXECUTABLE PROGRAM as the report type. The title will be visible when we start the report and can be edited later on as well. Let's title this report "My first ABAP report" as shown in Figure 1.2. Select SAVE to continue.

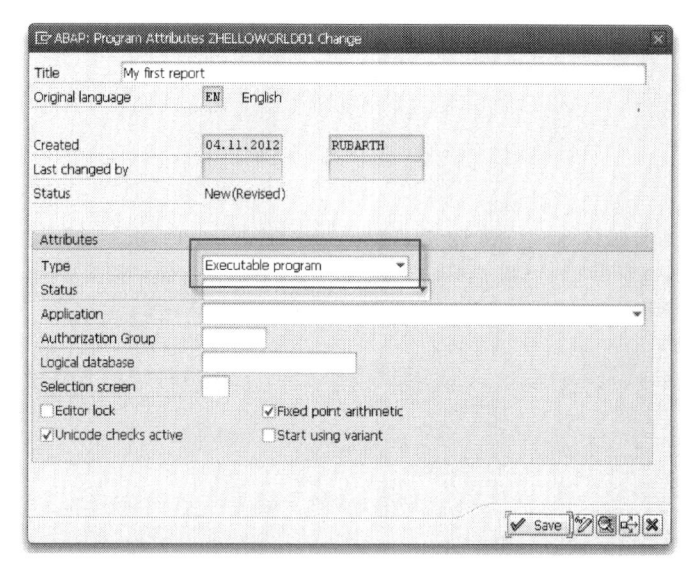

Figure 1.2: Program attributes for your first report

We aren't quite finished with attributes yet; the CREATE OBJECT DIRECTORY ENTRY window will pop up next, as shown in Figure 1.3.

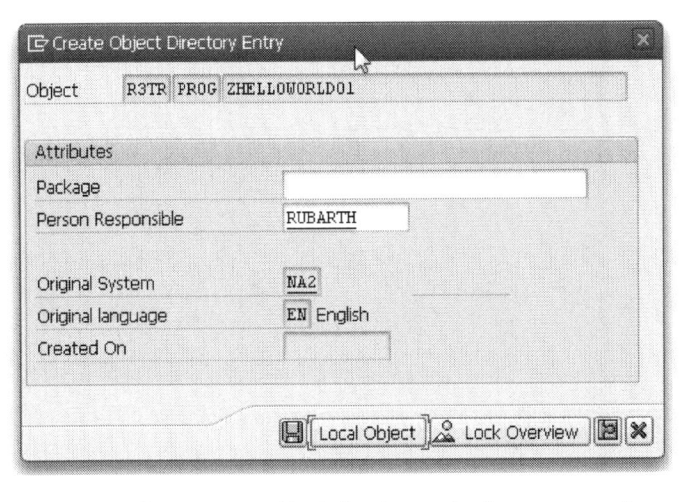

Figure 1.3: Creating an object directory entry for your report

Select the button LOCAL OBJECT and the popup will close. We will cover explanations of the *object directory* and the attribute *package* in subsequent chapters.

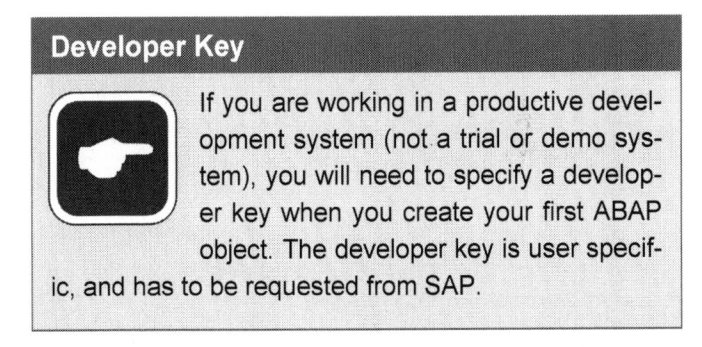

Developer Key

If you are working in a productive development system (not a trial or demo system), you will need to specify a developer key when you create your first ABAP object. The developer key is user specific, and has to be requested from SAP.

When the ABAP Editor pops up, you will see that the report already includes some code. As shown in Figure 1.4, the first few lines at the top are displayed in grey and start with an *asterisk* that precedes a comment. (The asterisk must be the first character of a line).

11

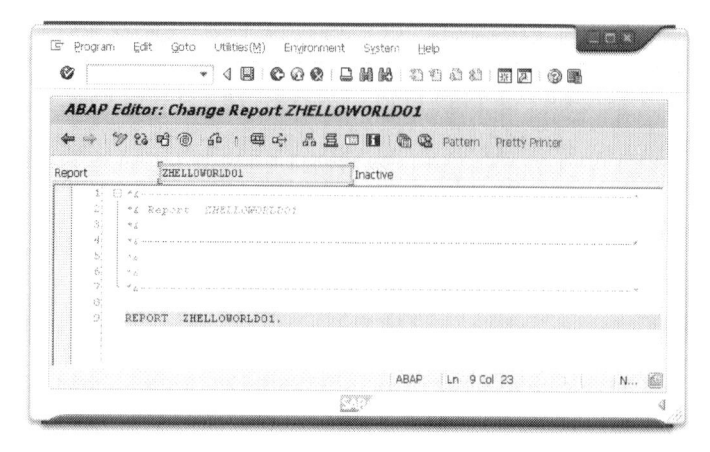

Figure 1.4: Initial code for your first report

Further down, the statement REPORT with the name of your first report is already entered (along with a period terminating the REPORT statement). This REPORT statement must precede each report.

> **Code Completion**
>
> Depending on the AS ABAP release you are using, the ABAP editor offers features such as *code completion* and *Intellisense* (starting with SAP BASIS 7.02). Since these features can be used similarly to other Integrated Development Environments (IDEs), it does not warrant explanation in this ABAP introduction.

Now you can complete your first report by entering the WRITE statement below the REPORT statement, so that the complete report contains just two (uncommented) lines:

```
REPORT ZHELLOWORLD01.
WRITE 'Hello world!'.
```

1.3 Starting the report

To save the report, either use the keyboard (Ctrl-S) or the save icon (right hand side beside the command field).

> **Central Development**
>
> ABAP development takes place in AS ABAP. That means that several developers can work simultaneously on their objects in a central development space. You do not have to deploy your ABAP objects to the server because they are automatically developed on the server.

Figure 1.5: Starting the report

Starting the report is as simple as saving it: use the icon DIRECT PROCESSING as shown in Figure 1.5 or the F8 function key. At first glance, the result is not surprising, see Figure 1.6.

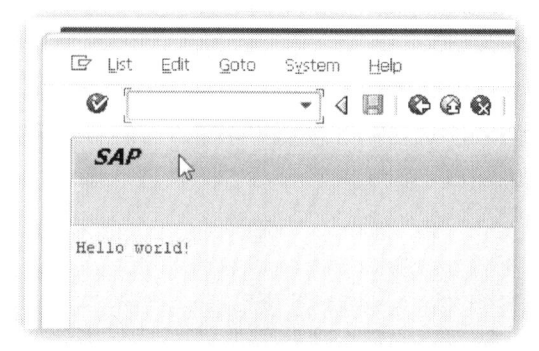

Figure 1.6: Output for your first report

You may wonder at this point why the title of the report is not displayed. A report not only needs to be saved, but needs to be activated in order to be complete and to show the title. If you take a second look at Figure 1.5, you will find the attribute "Inactive" following the name of the report.

Click on the ACTIVATION button (left hand side next to the start icon) and start the report again – now the title "My first ABAP report" is displayed as well.

Activating objects

As long as you do not activate a new report (or activate a change to an existing report), it is not relevant (or visible) to other users. This is important in a central development environment where you may work on objects that other developers use in their projects. Before activating your changes (which may impact other developers in their work), you can first check to see if the report still works without runtime errors and bugs.

When you start a version of your report that has not been activated, a compiled version is created. But this compiled version is used for the runtime of your user only – other users will work with the compiled version based on the activated code.

1.4 Using ABAP keyword documentation

ABAP keyword documentation is a comprehensive resource that explains ABAP statements with all of their options. Select the ABAP keyword WRITE in your report (with a single mouse click), and use the F1 function key to open the keyword documentation for the WRITE statement.

In the hit list (see Figure 1.7), double click the first entry to display the ABAP keyword documentation in a separate window.

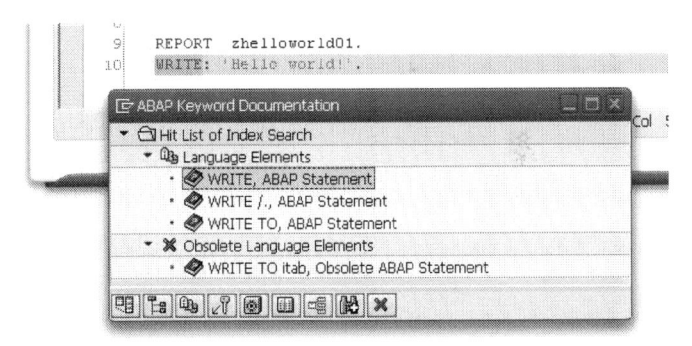

Figure 1.7: Starting the keyword documentation with F1

In the section EFFECT, you will find an explanation of the keyword selected. One of the explanations for the keyword WRITE is that the statement writes to the *list buffer*.

15

> **List buffer**
>
> The list buffer of a report is the memory area for recording screen lists. Reports use the list buffer as the standard output, which is displayed to the user at specific processing steps of the report – you may compare it to "stdout". But list buffers have more options, for example they can have several levels.

1.5 Viewing existing code

Most of SAP's business applications are developed in ABAP, and SAP delivers the source code with the applications. If you would like to look at standard code, here is the easy way to view it (explained for the application that you are working in), even if you do not know the name of the report or ABAP object type is used.

Use menu SYSTEM • STATUS to get general information about your system. Try this with your report: start the report, select the written text (list buffer) and use the menu SYSTEM • STATUS. You will see the report name, as demonstrated in Figure 1.8.

If you look at the field PROGRAM, and double click on the value ZHELLOWORLD01 the ABAP editor will display the code for your report. This is called *forward navigation*: double clicking on an object's name opens that object in the appropriate tool.

GETTING STARTED WITH ABAP

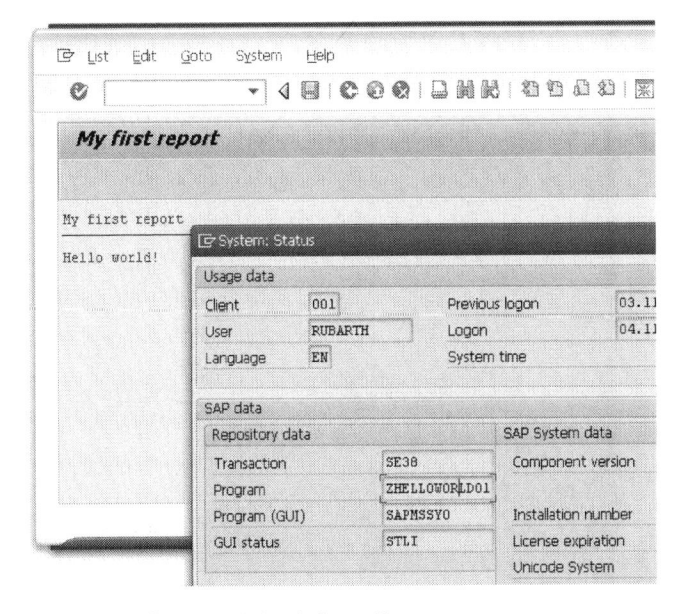

Figure 1.8: System status information

> **Forward Navigation**
>
> Forward navigation is general functionality available in the ABAP environment and works for other objects (and other tools) as well. If you double-click on the name of an object and it does not yet exist, the appropriate tool will propose that you create it.
>
> Forward Navigation takes a bit time of time to get used to since it deviates from the behavior of most text editors which highlight a word when it is double-clicked.

This kind of analysis and forward navigation works for other reports and transactions as well and offers an easy way to examine existing code.

> **Types of development**
>
> Apart from developing a new application, SAP customers and partners can also modify SAP's code or – even better – enhance the code.
>
> SAP offers the Enhancement Framework for this purpose. The big advantage is that SAP code enhancements will not get written over when SAP delivers an updated version of its code, for example with a Support Package that delivers corrections or legal updates.

1.6 Versioning your report

Activating your report does not automatically create a new version (in the sense that you have several versions in parallel). To have a fallback point for your code, you can generate a version for your report using the menu UTILITIES • VERSIONS... • GENERATE VERSION.

To get the list of existing versions, you use the menu entry UTILITIES • VERSIONS... • VERSION MANAGEMENT.

1.7 Conclusion

It's easy to get started with ABAP, either by viewing existing code or by creating your own report. The keyword documentation is a comprehensive resource for help. Now let's take a more detailed look at some typical coding statements.

2 Using ABAP Statements

Now let's take a closer look at ABAP statements, and expand our view to variables. In this chapter, readers will learn how to define variables and enable the user of a report to specify values for variables.

Debugging an application allows developers to follow the execution flow step by step in order to check the application. I will also introduce the ABAP debugger in this unit.

2.1 Using parameters as input variables

The statement PARAMETERS (always plural) is a simple way to allow users to provide input to a report that is stored in a variable. Specify the name of the parameter, its type, and if you would like a default value:

```
PARAMETERS pa_name type c length 12 DEFAULT 'HUGO'.
```

(In this example, we already used the type *c* for character which will be explained shortly, but yes: it is the type you expect it to be).

When you start the report, the system will display a simple input field with the given default value that you can overwrite, see Figure 2.1.

Figure 2.1: A parameter as an input variable

The parameter serves as an input field and as a variable.

Now let's use the input variable to make our welcome greeting a bit more personal, introducing chain statements as well:

```
WRITE: 'Hello', pa_name.
```

> **Chain statements**
>
> A chain statement combines several statements that use the same keyword into one statement that will be applied to several data objects. It requires a colon after the keyword (here: WRITE), and a comma between the data objects that the keyword applies to.

Did you try your own name with some lower case letters and find that they were displayed as upper case letters? You can use the *keyword addition* "lower case" for the PARAMETERS keyword to account for lower case letters. Note that this is not a *conversion* to lower case, but the permission for lower case letters (omit the conversion to upper case).

Still, the user interface (UI) in Figure 2.1 shows the name of the input variable, which is not always understandable to the user. If you consider that the length of a parameter name is restricted to 8 characters, you may want to include more meaningful text.

You can provide additional text for this variable by using the menu GOTO • TEXT ELEMENTS • SELECTION TEXTS. Enter "Your name" for the *selection text* of PA_NAME, as shown in Figure 2.2.

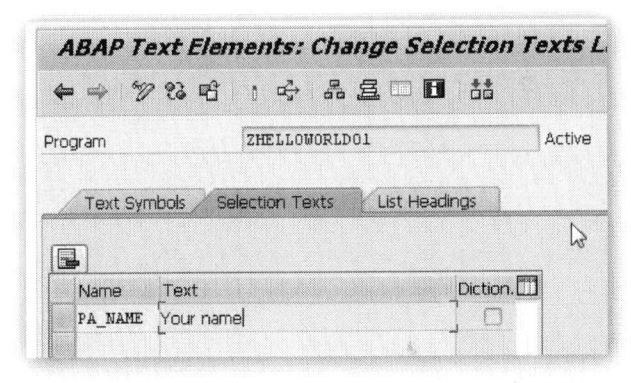

Figure 2.2: Maintenance of text for a parameter variable

It is important to note that you have to activate the selection text in this view before returning to the coding of your report (by using F3).

In the case that you have more than one object in an inactive state, the system will display these objects in a list. In this manner, you can selectively activate some of the objects, or all of them. In the following example, the report is inactive. When you activate the selection text both objects are part of the displayed list: object REPS (S for source), and object REPT (T for text), see Figure 2.3.

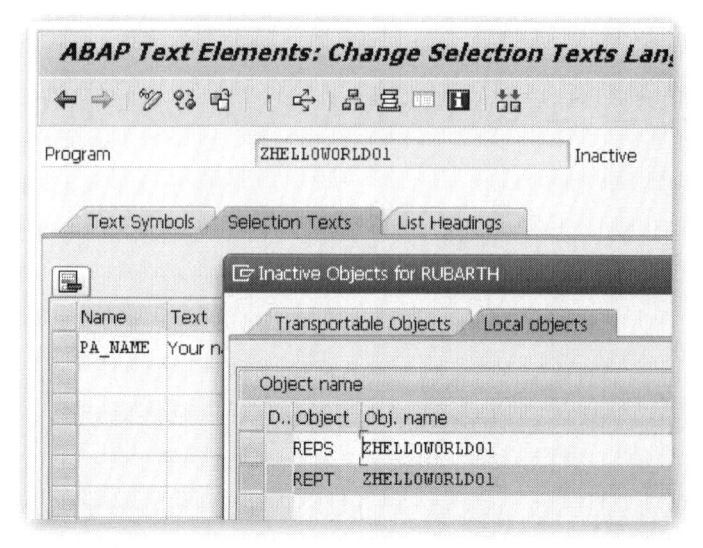

Figure 2.3: List of inactive objects

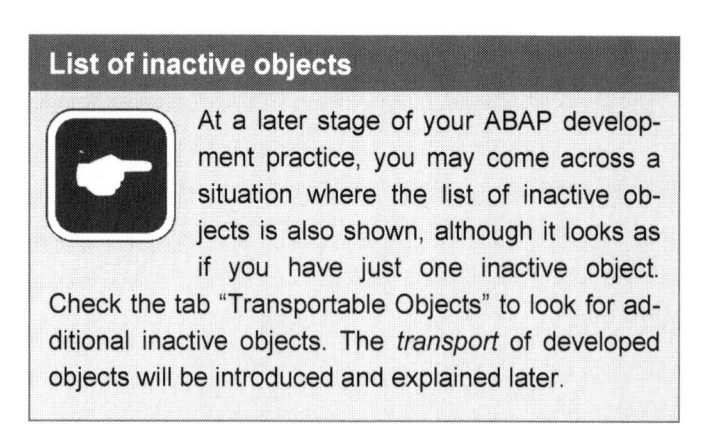

List of inactive objects

At a later stage of your ABAP development practice, you may come across a situation where the list of inactive objects is also shown, although it looks as if you have just one inactive object. Check the tab "Transportable Objects" to look for additional inactive objects. The *transport* of developed objects will be introduced and explained later.

The advantage of a selection text is that this text can be translated into other languages. If you choose a different language during log on, your report will show the text for the parameter in that language (assuming that the text was translated into that language).

> **Selection texts and selection screen**
>
> The parameter text is called "selection text" because it specifies the data selection. An advanced report that reads data from the database will have the following sequence: first the selection criteria have to be specified by the user (parameters statement), then the database access uses the selection criteria, and then the selected data are displayed to the user.
>
> The display of the selection texts is called the selection screen. The selection screen is assigned to the internal screen number 1000 and will be covered in more detail later.

To summarize:

▶ A PARAMETERS statement declares a local variable.

▶ At the beginning of the report, the selection screen displays an input field, so that the user can specify the value of the variable.

▶ The input field on the selection screen has a text label associated with it that can be translated.

2.2 Using conditional branches

Now let's look at using an IF statement to determine if the user has changed the default value for a parameter. Using an IF statement is easy. Remember – don't use any brackets and don't forget the period to complete the statement:

```
IF pa_name = 'HUGO'.
  WRITE 'Hello, are you really HUGO?'.
ELSEIF pa_name IS INITIAL.
  WRITE 'Please provide a name'.
ELSE.
  WRITE: 'Hello', pa_name.
ENDIF.
```

> **Assignment operator and equal sign**
>
> Please note that for the IF statement in the above example, the equal sign is not an assignment operator. This is different from other languages in which assignments and comparisons use different symbols.

In a similar way, the CASE statement can be used with logical expressions. We will use it in a later example, after we have looked at some elementary ABAP data types.

Language constructs that are similar to other languages include DO / ENDDO, as well as the WHILE / ENDWHILE block.

2.3 Using texts that can be translated

Of course it is a bad idea (and not best practice at all) to hard code strings because changing values afterwards means changing the code and translating the string is not possible. So let's use *text symbols* instead, which can be translated. Text symbols belong to your program exclusively, and are stored in a separate area – the *text pool* for the program. You have to use a three character alphanumerical ID to identify your text:

```
WRITE text-001.
```

Text symbols can be translated and their value is displayed in the logon language of the user in the user interface (the list buffer as the output of your report).

To define the value of the text symbol in your actual language, just double click the text symbol within your report. If the text symbol does not yet exist, a popup window will ask you whether you want to create the object. Select YES to confirm.

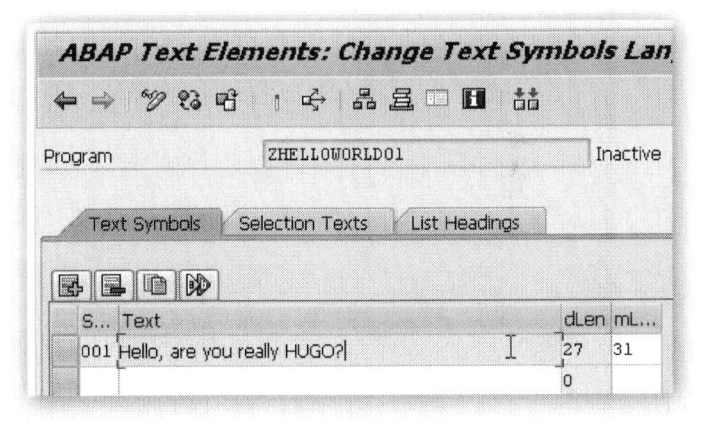

Figure 2.4: Maintaining text symbols

The maintenance view for text symbols (Figure 2.4) is the same as the one used for selection texts (Figure 2.2); only this time the first tab is used. Simply enter a value, and save it. You will be notified that the maximum length (column mLen in Figure 2.4) is automatically set.

Activate the text symbol and return to your code (function key F3). Now start your report again to confirm that the text symbol usage worked.

> **Text pool**
>
> You can also use the menu GOTO • TEXT-ELEMENTS • TEXT SYMBOLS to maintain the *text pool*: it is the list of text symbols in your report.

Remember: text symbols (like selection texts) have to be activated separately. They are not activated when you activate your report, although they are part of it.

2.4 Working with string variables

Now let's focus on string variables: a string is an elementary data object type (complex types will be discussed later).

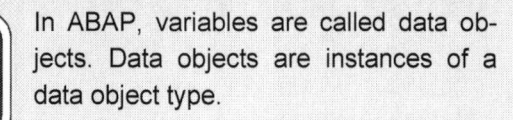

> **Data objects**
>
> In ABAP, variables are called data objects. Data objects are instances of a data object type.
>
> There are some predefined data object types in ABAP as in other languages, like string, integer, or Boolean.

A variable is defined with the statement DATA, followed by the name of the variable, and the type:

```
DATA l_msg type c length 12.
```

Type c is used for strings with a specific length. It is an incomplete data type since you have to specify the length. To assign a value, you use the equal sign:

```
l_msg = 'Please provide a name!'.
```

> **Naming convention**
>
> It is good practice to precede the data object name with an "l_" to show explicitly that it is a local variable. The variable is not visible in other reports or applications, so it can only be used locally in the report.
>
> A prefix is not required, but helpful when handling im/export parameters that are not local.

The default length is 1, like for most other incomplete data types. The DATA statement allows you to specify a default value as well, simply use the addition VALUE. And you can use the short form for defining a string by specifying the length in brackets directly after the name of the string:

```
DATA: l_msg(12) VALUE 'Please provide a name!'.
...
WRITE: l_msg.
```

Text symbols have the advantage that they can be translated, but string variables are used in cases where the value should be changed during the processing of the report.

2.5 Using elementary data types

Some of the elementary data types are character types (c for string, N for numeric text field, D for date, T for time) and numeric types (I for integer, F for floating point, P for packed).

The predefined elementary ABAP types with variable length are STRING (sequence of characters) and XSTRING for byte strings.

In addition, X is a hexadecimal ABAP type, which interprets individual bytes in memory.

> **The new data type decfloat**
>
> With the AS ABAP 7.02, SAP introduced a new data type *decfloat*. It combines the advantages of type packed (p) – which represents a decimal number precisely, but small value range – and the binary floating point number (f) – which has a large value range but cannot represent each decimal number precisely.

Let's look at type D as an example for understanding the ABAP internal variable format and the external variable display, which differs in some cases. "Internal" means values used during the runtime of the report; "external" means display of values to a user.

> **Predefined ABAP types and domains**
>
> Type D is a predefined type for a date, which is different from the *domain* DATE that is part of the *data dictionary* – both will be explained in a later section.
>
> Do not mix them up, especially for the following discussion of internal and external formats.

Use the PARAMETERS statement to define a new parameter pa_birth with a default value of year 1983, month 01, and day 23:

```
PARAMETERS: pa_birth type D default '19830123'.
```

Now start your report to confirm that the parameter is displayed in the user format that you have specified in your settings (menu SYSTEM USER • PROFILE • OWN DATA, tab DEFAULTS). The discrepancy between the internal data format and external representation is due to an automatic conversion by the ABAP runtime.

> **Conversion Routines**
>
> There are a number of conversion routines responsible for the conversion between the user interface (UI) and the ABAP internal display. It is important to remember this so that you do not assume that the values you see on the UI are the values that exist during runtime of your application. One way to check this is to debug your code and display the runtime values of data objects.

Let's now examine the CASE statement and some elementary ABAP data types in a new report called Z_MINI_CALC. The report takes two operands and one operator as input. The implementation of the report applies the operator on the operands with a mathematical operation. Two error situations should be considered and handled with writing an error text: division by zero, and the use of an unknown operator.

Start on your own and create this report (again as local object). You may wonder which data type to choose for the operands – let's start with integers. One possible approach is listed below, introducing the EXIT statement that ends the processing of the report (and displays the list buffer):

```
REPORT z_mini_calc.

PARAMETERS: pa_op1 TYPE i, pa_oper(1), pa_op2 TYPE i.
DATA: l_result TYPE i.

CASE pa_oper.
  WHEN '+'.
    l_result = pa_op1 + pa_op2.
  WHEN '-'.
    l_result = pa_op1 - pa_op2.
  WHEN '*'.
    l_result = pa_op1 * pa_op2.
  WHEN '/'.
    IF pa_op2 = 0.
      WRITE text-001.
      EXIT.
    ELSE.
      l_result = pa_op1 / pa_op2.
    ENDIF.
  WHEN OTHERS.
```

```
       WRITE text-002.
       EXIT.
    ENDCASE.
    WRITE: l_result.
```

Note that the result of each possible calculation is transferred to the local integer l_result, which is added to the list after the case statement is closed. The processing is stopped for the two error situations by writing an appropriate message to the list, and exiting the processing.

2.6 Debugging your report

To debug your report, use the menu PROGRAM • TEST • DEBUGGING, or set a breakpoint first and start the report as usual. To set (or release) a breakpoint, double-click the area in front of the respective line and the breakpoint sign displays. The icon for setting breakpoints can be used as well, as highlighted in Figure 2.5.

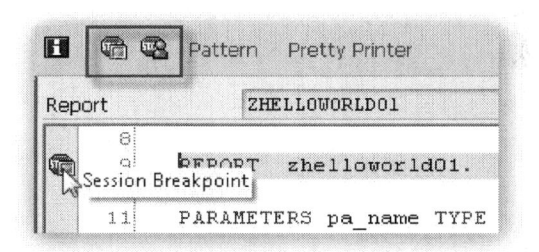

Figure 2.5: Setting breakpoints in your code

You can step through your code with the well-known debugging functions *single step*, *execute*, *return*, and *continue*.

> **Session and external breakpoints**
>
> Session breakpoints are valid for your user as long as your session is active. External breakpoints are valid for all users (SAP's new term for external breakpoints is user breakpoints).
>
> If you set a breakpoint during the debugging of your report, this breakpoint is only valid during the debugging session.

> **Command /h to start debugging**
>
> In situations where you want to debug a report *after* you have started it (for example on the selection screen), simply type "/h" in the command field and press enter. It will start the debugger as soon as you continue the processing of your report.

The default is now that the *new debugger* is used, separating debugger and debuggee in different modes. During the process, a separate session window will open (see Figure 2.6), and you can analyze the flow and the value of your data objects. A yellow arrow in front of the first line shows the point of processing.

To show the value for a variable, simply double-click on the data object, and the value will display below the tab VARIABLES 1. As you can see in the Figure 2.6, holding the mouse cursor above a variable name also displays the content (and the type).

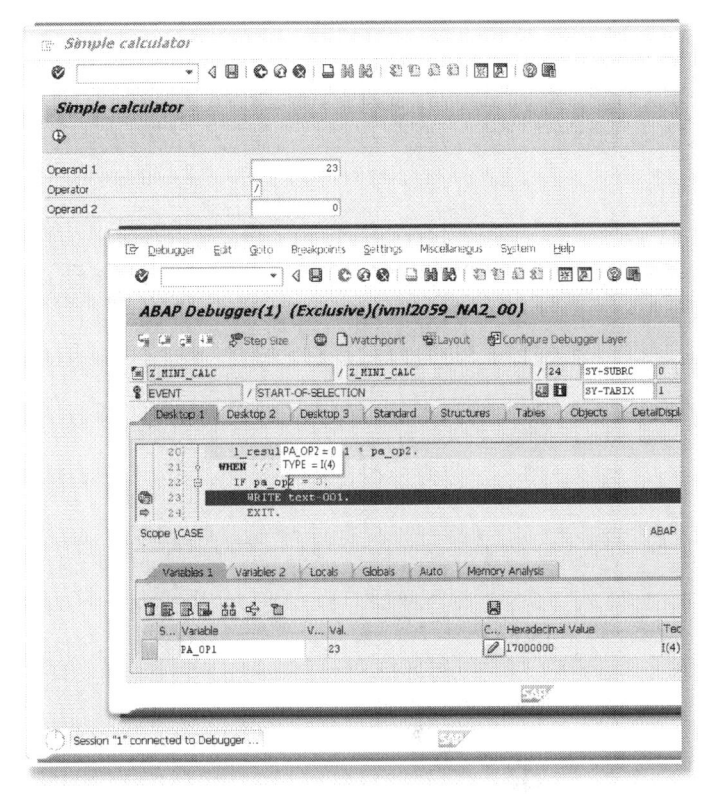

Figure 2.6: Debugging your report using the new debugger

Events for reports and debugging

You may have noticed that the debugger starts after the display of the selection screen. The reason is related to report events that we will not cover here. Events are one of the processing steps in the report, and one of the first events is AT SE-LECTION-SCREEN, which displays the selection screen. The debugging is effective after that (at event START-OF-SELECTION).

2.7 Conclusion

We have learned how easy it is to start with ABAP and how to ask the user of a report for input. Text used in a report has to be separated to allow for language-independent development, and debugging allows you to examine the flow of our report. Now it is time to expand the view from the ABAP editor, to the ABAP Workbench.

3 Using the ABAP Workbench

This chapter introduces the ABAP Workbench and explains the relationship between the ABAP Workbench and the development tools. We will take a closer look at the ABAP Editor, one of the most used tools in the ABAP Workbench. We will also look at how to customize some of the workbench features.

You can start a report without using the ABAP editor – if you know how to define a transaction code. Let's briefly cover how to define a transaction code.

3.1 Starting the ABAP Workbench

There are two ways to open the ABAP Workbench (also known as Object Navigator).

One option is to start the ABAP Workbench directly with transaction code SE80. Select the object to work on (for example your report) and then the Workbench will launch the appropriate tool (for reports, ABAP editor opens).

It works the other way as well: when you are working on your report using the ABAP editor, open the ABAP Workbench using the menu path UTILITIES • DISPLAY OBJECT LIST. This will open a separate area on the left hand side – as displayed in Figure 3.1 – which is called the object list.

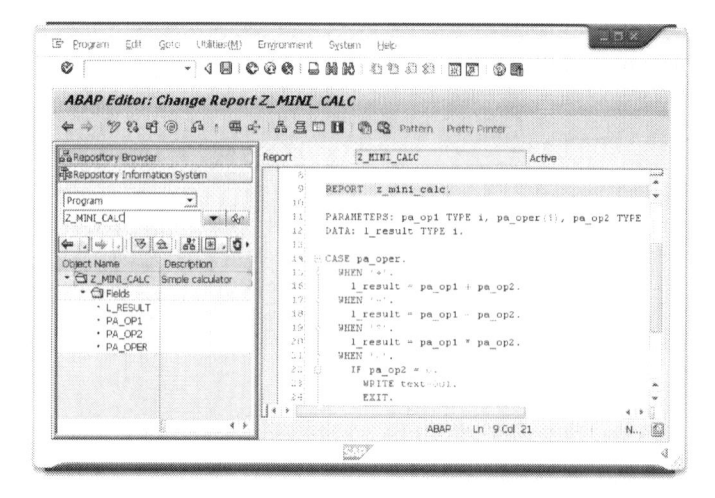

Figure 3.1: The object list for a report

The object list for a report shows the data objects used in the report.

You can not only open the object list in the ABAP editor, but also from each ABAP tool. The object list is a separate window section with its own navigation; it is not synchronized in all cases with the object displayed on the right hand side. You can always synchronize both sections, in one direction or the other: either use the menu path listed above to show the object list for an object displayed in the tool (right hand side). Or, select an object in the object list (left hand side) by double-clicking and it will display the appropriate tool on the right hand side of the screen. Later we will see that it can be useful not to have both sections synchronized.

Above the object list, three buttons with icons and text are visible: MIME REPOSITORY, REPOSITORY BROWSER (highlighted), and REPOSITORY INFOSYSTEM. Currently the REPOSITORY BROWSER is selected and below that, a drop down box shows PROGRAM and the name of our report.

Our report is part of the *ABAP repository*, like many other ABAP object types (for example ABAP classes) as well.

> **The ABAP Repository**
>
> All ABAP repository objects are stored in the database. When we save any changes for our report, the changes are written to the database, into the repository area in the database.
>
> Business data in the database are client-specific, since a client is a unit that is self-contained in terms of business, organization, and data. However, repository objects are client-independent: a report created in one client can be used in the other clients of that system as well. More than likely, the business results of the report are different when started in different clients, since the report will be working on different business data (which are client-specific).

You can change user-specific settings to determine which tools are displayed in the ABAP Workbench, as described in the following section.

3.2 Configuring ABAP Workbench options

The ABAP Workbench can display more tools than you will need in your daily work, so it is a good idea to display only the tools you need.

Select UTILITIES • SETTINGS to change your user-specific settings. The first tab WORKBENCH (GENERAL) allows you to set the BROWSER SELECTION of your choice. Use this tab to select only the REPOSITORY BROWSER and the REPOSITORY INFORMATION SYSTEM, as shown in Figure 3.2 below.

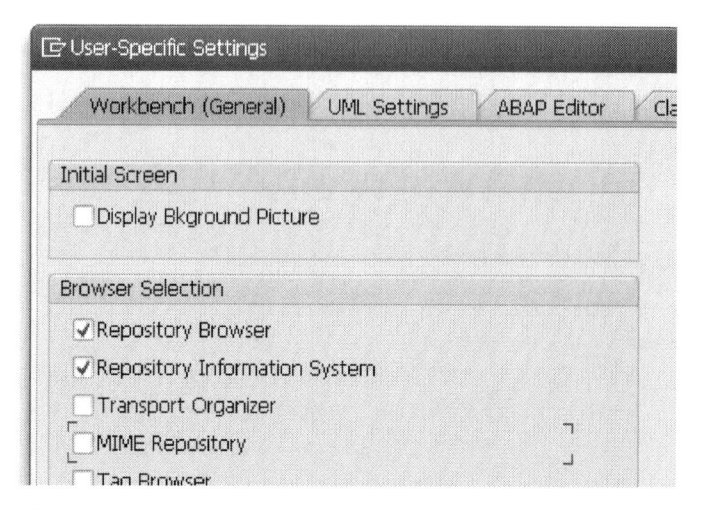

Figure 3.2: ABAP Workbench Settings

As you can see in the third tab, there is an area for user-specific settings for the ABAP EDITOR as well. Select that tab to see the PRETTY PRINTER tab, and use the CONVERT UPPERCASE/LOWERCASE option to select KEYWORD UPPERCASE, as shown in Figure 3.3.

After closing the popup window, use the PRETTY PRINTER button to automatically convert ABAP keywords to Uppercase (and to properly indent the lines, if you selected that option). These options optimize the display of your report according to your preferences, they are not relevant for the runtime of your report.

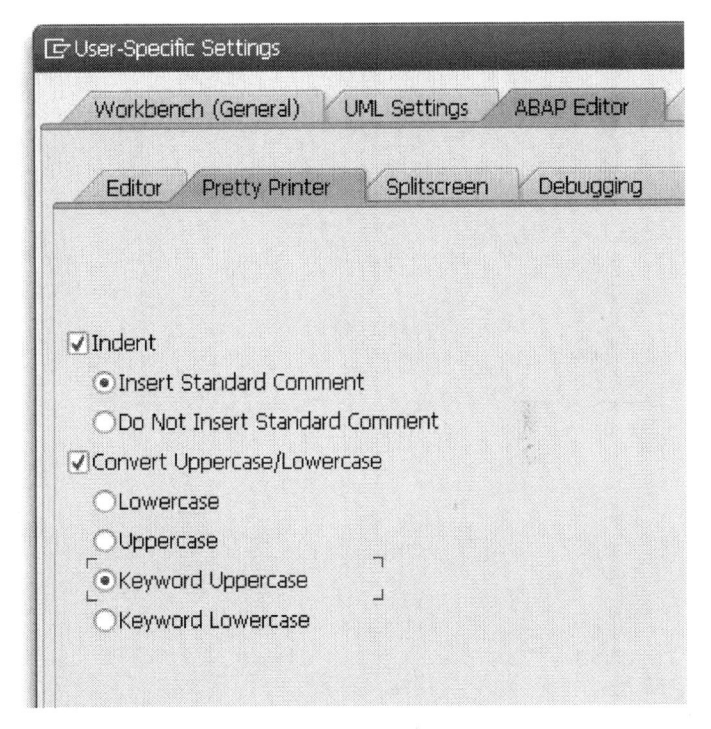

Figure 3.3: ABAP Editor settings for Pretty Printer

Now back to the selection PROGRAM in the REPOSITORY BROWSER: let's take a look at the drop down menu options.

3.3 Working with packages and transport requests

When you open the drop-down menu, you will see some of the existing repository object types, like REPORT and PACKAGE as displayed in Figure 3.4.

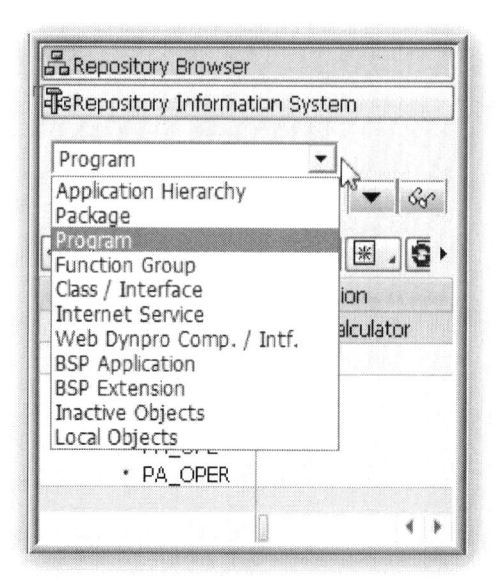

Figure 3.4: Repository object types in the Repository Browser

When we created our first report in Chapter 1, we skipped over an explanation of packages (Figure 1.3). Let's now examine packages in ABAP. Each object is assigned to a package, along with other objects that pertain to the same area of development, or business functionality. A package bundles different types of objects, like reports, UI objects, and ABAP classes, as long as they belong together from the application view. Several developers may work on the objects in one package.

Each ABAP object has another assignment that we previously skipped over: transport requests. A transport request bundles objects that will be transported together along the transport path.

> **ABAP Transports**
>
> ABAP objects are developed in a development system. When a development phase is done, the objects are transported to the next system (typically a quality assurance or test system). The third step in a typical transport landscape is a production system, in which no development is allowed.
>
> All three systems are separate installations of the AS ABAP, with their own system-id.

A transport request may include objects from different packages, and vice versa. Generally as a developer you do not have to worry about transports. As soon as you are done with the current development cycle, you will have to change all of your objects to status final (which is called "release your transport request"). Typically the project lead on your team will determine when to transport the objects. The transport is technically carried out by the AS ABAP (and its tools) as well.

To create a package, select the menu entry Package in the Repository Browser, and enter the name of your package, for example ZFIRSTPACKAGE. Press enter to display the package, and the ABAP Workbench will display a popup, asking whether you would like to create the (not yet existing) package.

Add a short description of the package, as displayed in Figure 3.5.

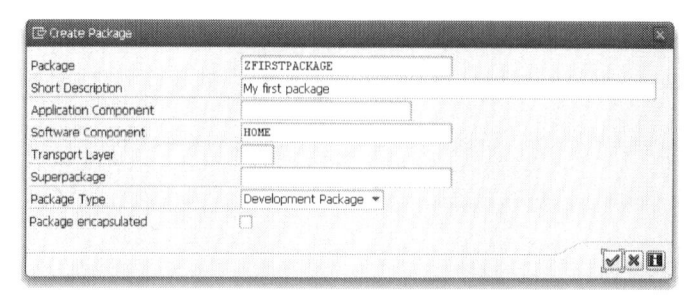

Figure 3.5: Creating a package

On the following screen (shown in Figure 3.6), you will either have to select an existing transport request to move the package into, or create a new one with the NEW icon.

Figure 3.6: Assigning a new package to a transport request

Now your package is created. The object list is still empty, but can include any new objects you create.

You can list all of your local objects by selecting LOCAL OBJECTS in the repository browser drop down menu (last entry), see Figure 3.4.

The following statements about packages and transport requests provide more information on the dependencies:

- All ABAP objects belong to a specific package
- Local objects belong to the package $TMP

- Local objects are local in the system in which they were created, they are not transported
- If you assign an object to your local objects, you do not assign a transport request to that object
- Typically you use $TMP for test objects which you do not want to transport to the productive ABAP system
- A transport typically includes objects from several users
- A transport request will typically include objects from several packages (but not from $TMP)

Local objects in package $TMP

When you created your first report, you did not specify a package or a transport request. By choosing "local object" (Figure 1.3), your report was automatically put into the package $TMP that contains all local objects. For this reason, you did not have to specify a package.

Local objects will not be transported to another system; they are kept local in the development system. That is why you did not have to specify a transport request.

"Local object" can have different interpretations: do not mix up local object concerning transports (like a report in $TMP that is not transported to another system) and local object concerning visibility of variables (like a local variable l_string that is only visible in the report in which it is declared).

> **Transporting a report creates a version**
>
> When you release the transport request for your report, a new version is created for the report.

3.4 Transaction code for a report

Each time you start your report, you first have to open the ABAP editor (transaction SE38). Starting the report is easier if you assign a transaction code to your report, which in turn can be entered in the command field to start it. Let's look at the creation of the transaction code to introduce an additional way to view or create objects: the Object Selection popup.

In the ABAP Workbench, use the button EDIT OBJECT to open the OBJECT SELECTION popup. You can either search for objects of various kinds, or create new objects. Use the icon next to the little scroll triangle to get a list of all the tabs available, each containing different object type choices (see Figure 3.7).

In the PROGRAM tab, select the radio button TRANSACTION and enter your transaction code, for example zmycalc (in the customer namespace, so starting with Z). Select the icon CREATE (F5) (as highlighted in Figure 3.7) to proceed.

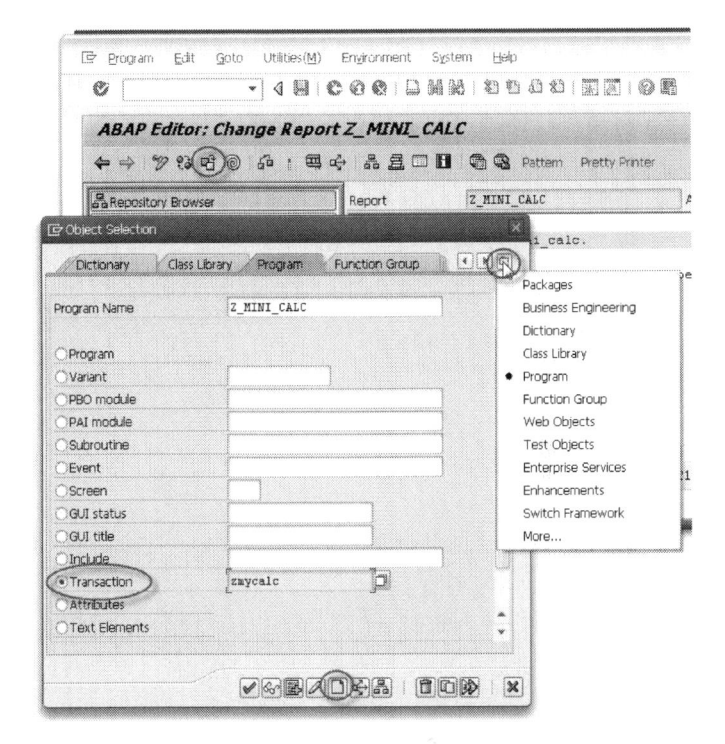

Figure 3.7: Using object selection popup to create a transaction code

In step 2, the next popup will ask you for transaction attributes. Enter a short text description, and in the START OBJECT section, select PROGRAM AND SELECT SCREEN (REPORT TRANSACTION), as demonstrated in Figure 3.8.

After closing the window, step 3 follows: assign the transaction code to your report Z_MINI_CALC, and set the GUI SUPPORT PARAMETER to SAPGUI FOR WINDOWS, as demonstrated at the bottom of Figure 3.9.

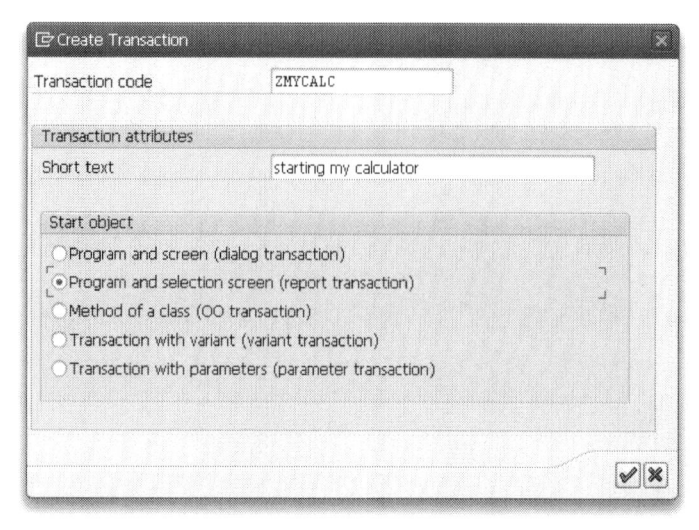

Figure 3.8: Creating a transaction code (step2)

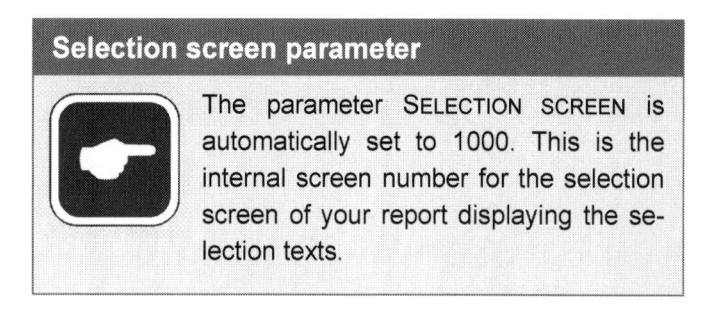

> **Selection screen parameter**
>
> The parameter SELECTION SCREEN is automatically set to 1000. This is the internal screen number for the selection screen of your report displaying the selection texts.

As soon as you have saved the transaction code (assigning it to your local objects again), it becomes part of the object list for your report, as you can see in Figure 3.9.

You can enter the transaction code into the command field to start your report, instead of opening the ABAP editor first. Or, you can create a favorite for the transaction code in the SAP Easy Access menu.

USING THE ABAP WORKBENCH

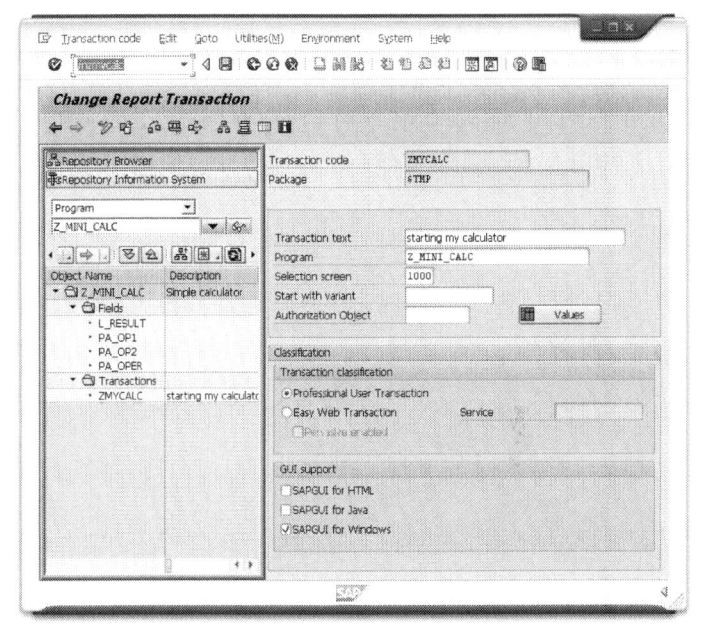

Figure 3.9: Assigning a transaction code to a report

49

4 Using data types from ABAP Data Dictionary (DDIC)

The data dictionary is a fundamental concept in ABAP. One of its most important uses is to provide global meta information for structures and tables. These global definitions can be reused in your application, which reduces application implementation effort. In addition, this chapter introduces internal tables as an important ABAP concept for handling large amounts of data in an application.

4.1 Getting started with complex data types

Imagine that you want to group several fields together, for example user data like name and address. Instead of working with separate simple data objects (variables), it is a good practice to combine these into a complex type: a structure variable that holds several fields of different types (and different name and length). The fields are often referred to as the *components* of the structure.

> **Nested structures**
>
> Structures can be nested, which means that a structure may also contain a component that is a structure (instead of a single field), which is then a sub-structure. That is why it is more precise to call them structure components instead of structure fields.

A complex data object is often used as an import or export object during the call of a function module or class method (instead of passing several fields separately), as we will see in the following chapter about modularization techniques.

You can define a complex type (a structure) in your report, which is a local definition. Or, you can define and use global definitions as part of the ABAP Data Dictionary, as we will see in the next section.

The local definition of a complex type uses the keyword TYPES, and lists the fields with their types and names. Again the statement (covering 7 lines in this case) is closed with a period:

```
TYPES: BEGIN OF lty_address,
  city(40) TYPE c,
  zipcode(5) TYPE n,
  country(40) TYPE c,
  street(50) TYPE c,
  number(5) TYPE n,
END OF lty_address.
```

Here, the prefix "lty_" indicates that it is a local definition type.

Note that the TYPE statement can also be used to define a single field (simple data type) instead of a structure, for example a character with a length of 40.

After a structure type is declared, it can be referenced to create a complex data object – or several, if necessary:

```
DATA: ls_address TYPE lty_address,
      ls_address_ext type lty_address.
```

The prefix "ls_" expresses that the complex data object resembles a *local structure*.

To access a field, for example to set a value for the field street, combine the name of the structure (ls_address) with the name of the field (street), connected with a minus sign:

```
ls_address-street = 'Neurottstrasse'.
```

Assume that you have two different structures that have some components (fields) with identical names and types, and you want to pass the values from one structure to the other. You will not have to pass all of the fields manually, which may be a lot of work for structures with many fields. The ABAP statement MOVE-CORRESPONDING copies the contents of the source structure components to the target structure components for those with identical names:

```
MOVE-CORRESPONDING ls_address TO ls_address_ext.
```

> **Structure definition using DATA**
>
> Note that you can use the keyword DATA instead of TYPE to simultaneously define a type and create an instance for a structure. But this does not allow reusing the structure definitions for additional structure instances.

Let's summarize the information thus far on structures with an example where a structure is used for the fields of an address. The code contains the following steps:

53

Using Data Types from ABAP Data Dictionary (DDIC)

1. Local declaration of a complex data object type
2. Definition of two structures, based on the local type
3. Filling the first structure with address data
4. Copying the data to the second structure
5. Changing two fields of the second structure

```
REPORT  z_structure_demo.

* 1. Local declaration of a complex data object type
TYPES: BEGIN OF lty_address,
  city(40) TYPE c,
  zipcode(5) TYPE n,
  country(40) TYPE c,
  street(50) TYPE c,
  number(5) TYPE n,
END OF lty_address.

* 2. Definition of three structures and one internal
    table, based on the local type
DATA: ls_address TYPE lty_address,
      ls_address_ext TYPE lty_address.

* 3. Filling the first structure with address data
ls_address-city = 'Walldorf'.
ls_address-zipcode = '69190'.
ls_address-country = 'Germany'.
ls_address-street = 'Hasso-Plattner-Ring'.
ls_address-number = 20.

* 4. Copying the data to the second structure
MOVE-CORRESPONDING ls_address TO ls_address_ext.
```

```
* 5. Changing two fields of the second structure
ls_address_ext-street = 'Dietmar-Hopp-Allee'.
ls_address_ext-number = 14.
```

But instead of creating a local type definition in your application, it is easier to reuse existing types from the data dictionary, as shown in the next section.

4.2 Working with the ABAP Data Dictionary (DDIC)

The ABAP Data Dictionary (DDIC) is the central repository where data types can be defined (and found) to reuse in any application. The most important objects in the DDIC are structures, tables, data elements, and domains.

You can access the DDIC from the ABAP Workbench (SE80), or by starting the tool directly with transaction code SE11, which will show the Data Dictionary selection screen (see Figure 4.1).

Let's look up the structure SYST as an example in DDIC. Enter the name SYST in the first field DATABASE TABLE , and choose DISPLAY to display the definition of SYST. This structure contains more than 170 fields (although some of them are marked as obsolete).

A structure consists of fields (called components in the DDIC too). A structure's fields are given a name and they reference a data type (called component type in the DDIC).

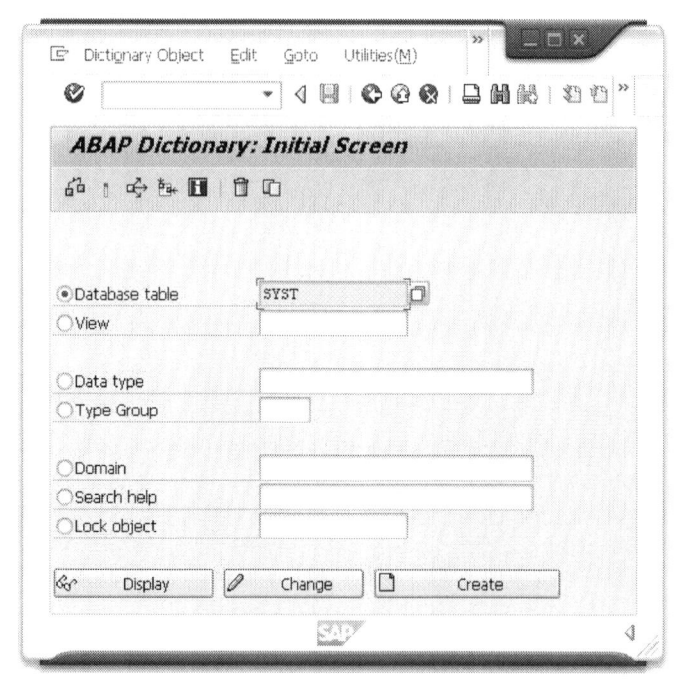

Figure 4.1: Data dictionary (DDIC) selection screen

Let's take a closer look at the first line of structure SYST (see Figure 4.2), which is the first field (or component) of the structure. The field is called INDEX, and references the data type SYINDEX.

You can double click the name SYINDEX to see the definition of that data type in the DDIC (visible in Figure 4.2 as well: the window in foreground with title "Dictionary: Display Data Element").

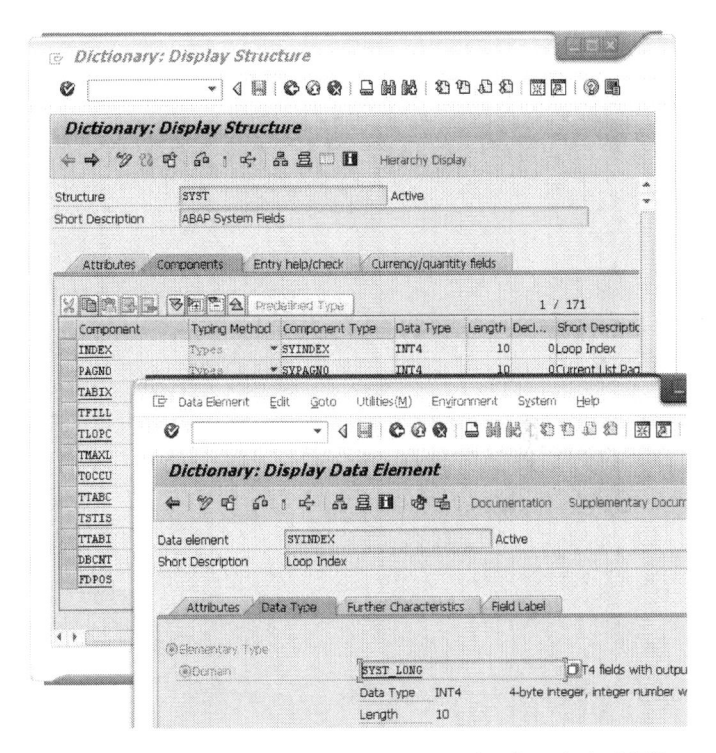

USING DATA TYPES FROM ABAP DATA DICTIONARY (DDIC)

Figure 4.2: A structure, a data element, and a domain in DDIC

How is the domain different than the data element? The domain provides the technical attributes, like integer of length 4. The data element includes semantically important information. Two data elements can refer the same domain, but can have different semantics as we will see in the next DDIC example: a transparent table definition.

57

USING DATA TYPES FROM ABAP DATA DICTIONARY (DDIC)

> ### Structure SYST is used for runtime object SY
>
> The structure SYST is important, as it is used as a type for the complex data object SY. During runtime of an application (for example our report), SY is made available by the ABAP runtime (without separate declaration), and it contains important runtime information.
>
> A good example is the field SY-SUBRC that contains the return code of the last ABAP statement. It is also displayed prominently when using the debugger (see Figure 2.6).

Return to the initial screen of the DDIC, and specify SFLIGHT in the first field DATABASE TABLE. Choose DISPLAY to display the definition as shown in Figure 4.3.

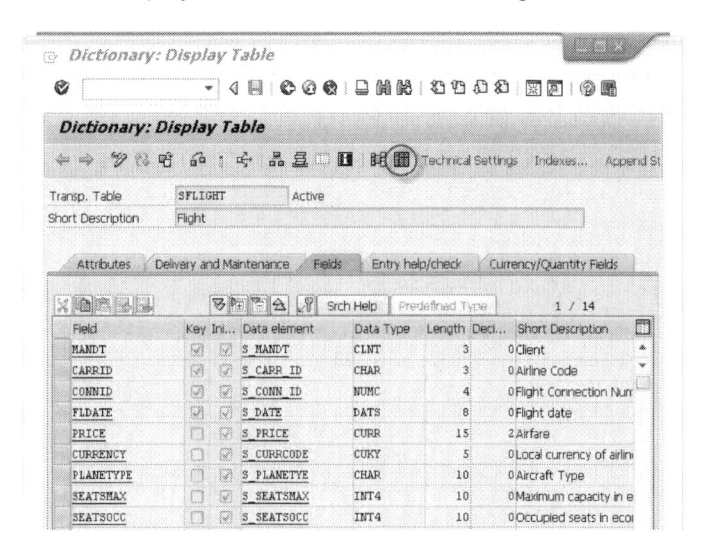

Figure 4.3: Transparent table SFLIGHT in DDIC

USING DATA TYPES FROM ABAP DATA DICTIONARY (DDIC)

> **Flight model**
>
> SFLIGHT is part of the flight model, a demo application delivered by SAP. The flight model consists of several ABAP objects and is based on flight connections between cities, offered by several airlines.

A transparent table is very similar to a structure definition: they both list fields (with names and references to data elements), and can be referenced in an application as a type for complex data objects (like a structure or an internal table, as discussed in the next section).

Before discussing the difference between structures and transparent tables, let's first finish comparing domains and data elements. In Figure 4.3, you see the two components SEATSMAX and SEATSOCC. Both are variables of type integer with length 4 (based on the domain S_SEATS, not shown here). But the two components have different semantic meanings. It makes a difference for an airplane if four seats out of 800 are occupied, or if it just has four seats at all – which may be significant for the pilot as well.

The big difference between a DDIC structure and a DDIC transparent table is that a transparent table is used for the structure (meta information) of a *database* table. If you compare Figure 4.2 and Figure 4.3, you will find a button for a transparent table (highlighted in Figure 4.3) that is not displayed for a structure. This button leads directly from the display of the transparent table to the Data Browser, showing the *content* of the associated database table. You can of course open the Data Browser independently with transaction code SE16.

So a transparent table defines a structure which is the foundation of a database table. The database table contains business content on the database layer, and the transparent table does not contain business content, just the meta information for it.

If you want to work on business data in a table on the application level (in your report), you will have to use an internal table. I will explain this in the following section.

> **Customer Namespace in DDIC**
>
> Objects created by a customer need the prefix ZZ to reside in the customer namespace (instead of Z like for a report).

> **Entity Relationship Model (ERM) in DDIC**
>
> Relational data models – reflecting the relationship of business units in the relationship of database tables – can also be created or viewed in the DDIC.

4.3 Working with internal tables

In our report, we can use simple data objects (single fields) and complex data objects (structures as a sequence of fields) as data objects with values during runtime on the application level.

USING DATA TYPES FROM ABAP DATA DICTIONARY (DDIC)

> **Three tier architecture of AS ABAP**
>
> A simple way to think about ABAP architecture is as three levels: the *database level* with the database containing the business data in a persistent manner, the *application level* on which the ABAP applications (like reports) are executed (runtime), and the *presentation level* on which the user interface resides.

Another important complex data object for values during runtime is an internal table.

An internal table is a table in the sense that each line has the same structure (the same sequence of fields). That is why you can easily define an internal table by referencing a structure type with the keyword TYPE TABLE OF:

```
DATA: lt_addresses TYPE TABLE OF lty_address.
```

Again the prefix "lt_" expresses that the complex data object resembles a *local (internal) table*. Some developers even use the prefix "itab_" for such complex data objects.

The definition of an internal table can of course reference a structure or a transparent table definition from the DDIC, so that you may not have to define a local structure first.

Internal tables only exist on the application level during the runtime of an application, so they are only visible internally in the application in which they were created.

They are different from database tables which contain business data on the database level, and which are generally available for all applications.

Of course it is possible to read data from a database table into an internal table, we will cover this topic in a subsequent chapter

To work with the content of an internal table, you need an additional data object with the same line type: a structure. This structure is often called a work area because in that structure, you work with the data of one table line. You cannot access the fields of the internal table directly, so you need to copy the fields of the appropriate table line into the structure and can access the fields of the structure in the usual way.

The declaration was already introduced; it looks similar to the declaration of the table:

```
DATA: lt_addresses type table of lty_address,
      wa_address type lty_address.
```

Some developers set the prefix of the structure that acts as work area to "wa_" to make the role more prominent.

Finally, you need a loop that will use the table and the work area: for each loop pass, the next line of the table is copied into the work area. This is possible with the statement LOOP AT <table> INTO <work area>. Now inside the loop, you can write the content of the structure fields:

```
LOOP AT lt_addresses INTO wa_address.
   WRITE: wa_address-city,
          wa_address-zipcode,
```

```
    ...
    .
ENDLOOP.
```

You can add a condition to the LOOP AT statement (WHERE number = 14) to select only a part of the internal table.

Let's build on the concept of the simple report on structures from the last section (Z_STRUCTURE_DEMO) by defining an internal table, appending both structures to the table, and writing the content of the table to the list (continuing the step numbering from above):

6. Define an internal table and a structure as a work area

7. Append the two existing structures to the internal table

8. Write the fields of all table lines on the list using a loop

```
* 6. Define an internal table and a structure as
     work area
DATA: wa_address TYPE lty_address,
      lt_addresses type table of lty_address.

* 7. Append both structures to the internal
     table
APPEND ls_address TO lt_addresses.
APPEND ls_address_ext TO lt_addresses.

* 8. Write the fields of all table lines on the
     list using a loop
LOOP AT lt_addresses INTO wa_address.
```

```
WRITE: / wa_address-city,
         wa_address-zipcode,
         wa_address-country,
         wa_address-street,
         wa_address-number.
ENDLOOP.
```

Notes:

▶ For clarity of your coding, you should bundle all DATA declarations on the top of the report, but you do not have to.

▶ The slash for the WRITE statement creates a new line for each table entry.

Table keys for internal tables

An internal table can have keys if you used a transparent table for the definition of the internal table (instead of a structure). The table keys may be used for some of the statements listed below. Remember that a transparent table in the DDIC contains the meta information for a structure object, including keys.

The following overview lists the ABAP statements that can be used to work on an internal table (the keyword documentation provides more details):

USING DATA TYPES FROM ABAP DATA DICTIONARY (DDIC)

```
LOOP AT lt_addresses INTO ls_address ...
READ lt_addresses INTO ls_address ...
MODIFY TABLE lt_addresses FROM ls_address ...
INSERT ls_address INTO TABLE lt_addresses ...
DELETE lt_addresses ...
APPEND ls_address TO lt_addresses.
```

Apart from the APPEND statement, all of them can be used with a condition.

To wrap up, let's reuse a transparent table from DDIC for an internal table. This demonstrates the benefit of the DDIC: the entry help for table fields is useful for PARAMETERS as well.

```
REPORT  z_demo_table.

PARAMETERS: pa_carid TYPE sflight-carrid,
            pa_conid TYPE sflight-connid.

DATA: ls_flight TYPE sflight,
      lt_flights TYPE TABLE OF sflight,
      l_num TYPE i.

ls_flight-carrid = pa_carid.
ls_flight-connid = pa_conid.

APPEND ls_flight TO lt_flights.
APPEND ls_flight TO lt_flights.

DESCRIBE TABLE lt_flights LINES l_num.

WRITE: l_num.
```

Notes:

- The report does not do anything beneficial, apart from give you some insight into the advantages of DDIC.

- On the selection screen, use the F4 help on the second parameter first: the first parameter will be filled as well.

- Examine the transparent table SFLIGHT in the DDIC again (transaction code SE11), check the tab ENTRY HELP/CHECK (visible in Figure 4.3 as well).

- The statement DESCRIBE TABLE is used to count the lines of the table.

5 Modularization and reusing functionality

It is a good practice in all development environments to use modularization techniques, so that code can be reused and the application sequence stays transparent. This chapter will introduce the three most important modularization techniques in ABAP: forms, function modules, and ABAP classes.

Each of the modularization techniques share a commonality: they bundle statements into a module. The coding module has an interface to exchange variables between the outer part (the caller of the module) and the inner part (the module implementation).

This chapter will introduce each modularization technique and how to use them. Simple test procedures for the modules are explained where applicable.

5.1 Using form routines

Form routines are a technique for local program modularization, the coding of the form can only be reused in the program in which it was created.

A form routine is also called a subroutine: it bundles a sequence of statements together and has an interface to pass variables.

5.1.1 Defining form routines

You define a form routine in your report with the statements FORM and ENDFORM. The FORM statement lists the variables by their types, either by TABLES (for internal tables), by USING (for import variables only), or by CHANGING (for import and export parameters):

```
FORM mycalc
         TABLES my_itab TYPE table
         USING operand1 TYPE i
               operand2 TYPE i
               operator TYPE c
         CHANGING result TYPE i.
* coding of form routine ...
ENDFORM.
```

Note that the name of the form does not have to be in the customer namespace (prefix "Z" or "Y") because it is not a separate ABAP object: it belongs to a report. The TABLES specification was listed for completeness, but will not be used further in our example.

The coding in the form (the implementation) will be similar to the coding of our Z_MINI_CALC report:

```
FORM mycalc USING operand1 TYPE i
                  operand2 TYPE i
                  operator TYPE c
            CHANGING result TYPE i.
  CASE operator.
    WHEN '+'.
      l_result = operand1 + operand2.
```

```
      WHEN '-'.
        l_result = operand1 - operand2.
      WHEN '*'.
        l_result = operand1 * operand2.
      WHEN '/'.
        IF operand2 = 0.
          WRITE text-001.
          EXIT.
        ELSE.
          l_result = operand1 / operand2.
        ENDIF.
      WHEN OTHERS.
        WRITE text-002.
        EXIT.
    ENDCASE.
  ENDFORM.
```

When you create the form and use the pretty printer, some commented lines will be added prior to the form. You can enter some explanations there as documentation for the form.

If you have reused your report, the text symbols should have been maintained, otherwise you will have to take care of that.

As you see, the form is allowed to write text to the list, which is used for the two error situations (division by zero, and wrong operator). Still, it is questionable if this is the purpose of the form, or if error situations should be handled from the caller.

5.1.2 Calling form routines

The call form routine uses the statement PERFORM with the name of the form routine, and the actual parameters to be passed to the form routine:

```
PERFORM mycalc
USING pa_op1 pa_op2 pa_oper
CHANGING l_result.
```

As you can see, the variable names do not have to match the name in the definition, as the sequence of the variable is relevant.

When you now return to the report Z_MINI_CALC, you can add the calculation to the form, and call the form:

```
REPORT z_mini_calc.
PARAMETERS: pa_op1 TYPE i,
            pa_oper(1), pa_op2 TYPE i.
DATA: l_result TYPE i.

PERFORM mycalc USING pa_op1 pa_op2 pa_oper
CHANGING l_result.
WRITE: l_result.
```

Of course it is not beneficial if you just have one call form routine in your report – reusing is beneficial when the form will be used several times.

Now when you execute the report, you might not see a big difference. But think about the "division by zero" case: the form routine can write text to the list, but the EXIT statement just leaves the form, and the processing is continued. You can think about alternative solutions for that: one possibility is to return the error text inside the result parameter. Another way is to add another form parameter that is filled with a text in error situations, and it has to be handled by the caller. Let's see later how other reuse techniques deal with the same situation.

> **Passing variables that cannot be changed in the routine**
>
> If you want to pass a variable to the routine, but want to avoid the routine changing the variable, you can pass the *value* of the variable instead of the variable itself:
>
> `PERFORM mycalc USING value(l_op1) ...`

Form routines are only listed in this introduction so that you are able to analyze existing code, but it is not best practice to start working with form routines. They cannot be reused in other reports, they do not have a transparent interface handling, and they do not have dedicated error handling. And form routines are an ABAP technique that SAP has identified as obsolete and it should not be used any longer.

5.2 Using function modules

5.2.1 Understanding the basics of function modules

Function modules contain functionality that can be reused globally, i.e. from within any application in the system. The modules are defined in the function builder (instead of locally in a report) and are stored in the ABAP Repository.

A function module is not associated with one specific report, but with a *function group*. A function group bundles several function modules that are a part of the same area of development or business area. (The hierarchy level above a function group is a package.)

The call of a function module will exchange parameters between the report and the function module according to the defined interface (exchange parameters defined in the function module), as depicted in Figure 5.1.

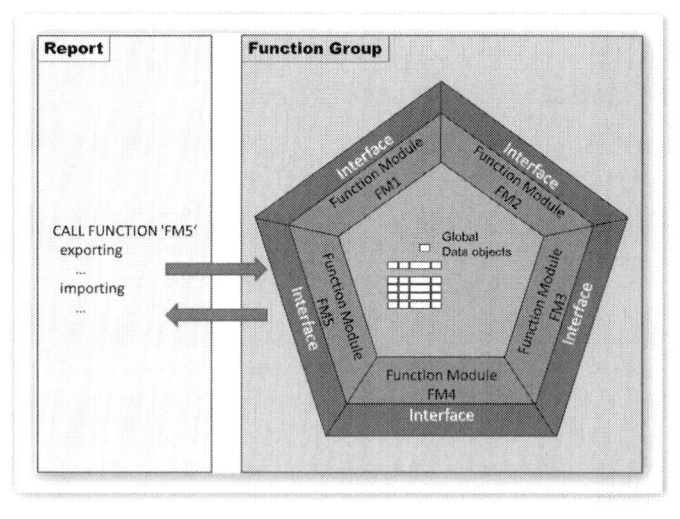

Figure 5.1: Principle of function module call

There are more than 100,000 function modules available in an ABAP system, so it is important to take reuse techniques into consideration when you start to develop your own application.

Function modules may include any ABAP statement, for example an arithmetic calculation. It is important to indicate that function modules delivered by SAP (or by SAP partners) may include database operations (read and/or write) as well. So even if you are not familiar with database access techniques (these are discussed later), you can read database tables by reusing function modules.

> **Database changes with function modules**
>
> ❗ For database changes, you can use existing function modules as well. The advantage is that these modules already include all necessary steps (for example authorization check, consistency check, and setting a lock). Still one important step may be required: a separate COMMIT WORK statement.

Some function modules are remote enabled and can be called remotely (outside of the ABAP system). The caller can be another ABAP system, or even a non-ABAP application. These remote-enabled function modules are a subset of all function modules.

Furthermore, a subset of the remote-enabled function modules are special, dedicated function modules. They act as Business-APIs to access the ABAP system and are called BAPIs (Business-API).

The hierarchy of function module types is shown in Figure 5.2.

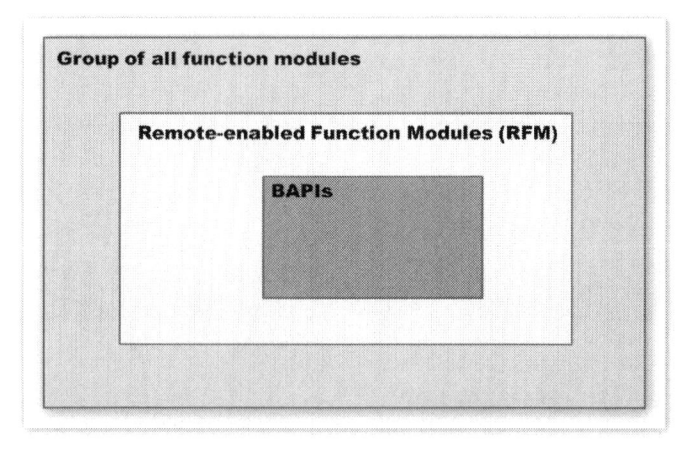

Figure 5.2: Function modules, RFM, and BAPIs

> **User interfaces in function modules**
>
> Some function modules may even create a dialog (a user interface) instead of just exchanging parameters with the calling application. This will be displayed in the SAPGUI window (session) of the user that started the application. For a remote call to an RFM, this will not work because there is no SAPGUI window to display the dialog. So an RFM should not include a user interface.
>
> User interface techniques will be discussed in a subsequent section.

5.2.2 Examining existing function modules

So let's use the function builder (transaction code SE37) to look at an example of a function module and examine the implementation (the coding), as well as the interface of the function module.

Figure 5.3 shows the initial function builder screen, that will ask you to specify (or search for) the name of the function module that you want to work on.

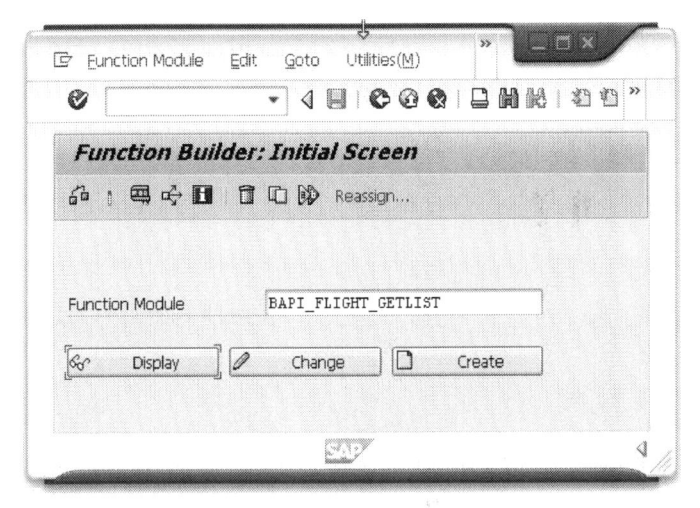

Figure 5.3: Initial screen of the function builder

After specifying the name of the function module (in this case it is BAPI_FLIGHT_GETLIST – part of the flight model), choose DISPLAY. Initially, the source code of the function module is displayed. The source code of a function module (like for nearly all other ABAP objects) is delivered with AS ABAP and can be viewed and examined.

Several of the tabs shape the function module interface (mainly IMPORT, EXPORT, TABLES, and EXCEPTIONS). The first tab shows the ATTRIBUTES of the function module, as you can see in Figure 5.4.

The first attribute listed is the *function group,* which the function module belongs to. Function modules that belong to the same (business) area are bundled in a function group. The function group again is part of a package, which is displayed under GENERAL DATA, visible in Figure 5.4 as well.

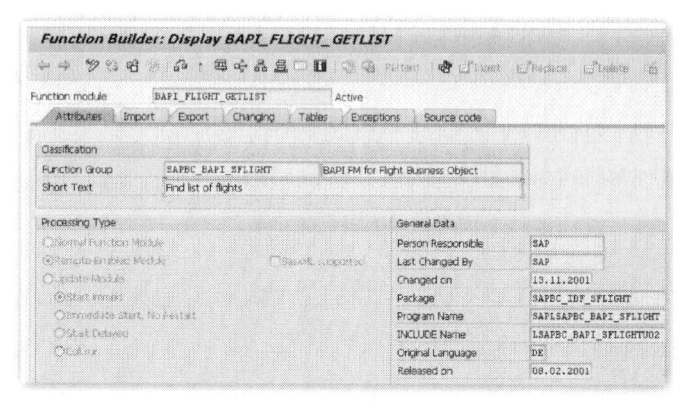

Figure 5.4: Function module attributes

Another important attribute is the PROCESSING TYPE. If that attribute is set to REMOTE-ENABLED MODULE, the function module can be accessed remotely, as mentioned above.

Abbreviations RFM and RFC

The functionality (module design) that can be executed remotely is the *remote enabled function module.* The common abbreviation for *remote enabled function module* is **RFM**. The module *call* (during runtime) to execute the RFM is the *remote function call*, also known as **RFC**.

76

The interface defines which data objects can be exchanged between the calling application and the function module. The primary parts of the function module interface are:

- ▶ IMPORT parameters (fields or structures) that are imported into the function module

- ▶ EXPORT parameters (fields or structures) that are passed back from the module after the execution

- ▶ TABLES parameters that are special as they can be used to transfer internal tables in both directions (import and export)

- ▶ EXCEPTIONS that lists predefined error cases

> **TABLES and variable usages**
>
> Note that not all function modules really use the TABLES data objects in both directions, some just return a table object. It depends on the function module functionality if the table is really imported and used in the code.

If you check the declaration of a variable on the tab IMPORT (Figure 5.5), you see that it can be typed with a reference to the dictionary (column ASSOCIATED TYPE). This makes sense: the DDIC type can be referenced by the calling application as well, which will avoid errors due to passing the wrong data type to the function module. Note that for RFMs, all variables *have* to be typed with reference to the dictionary.

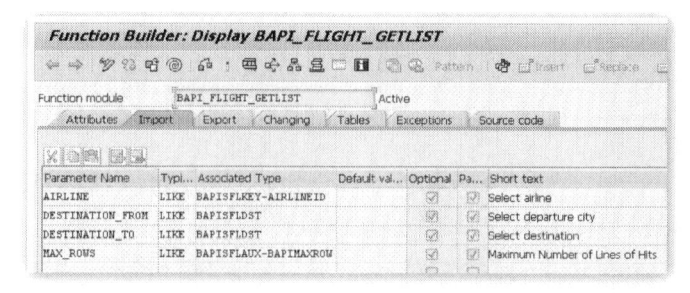

Figure 5.5: Function module import parameters

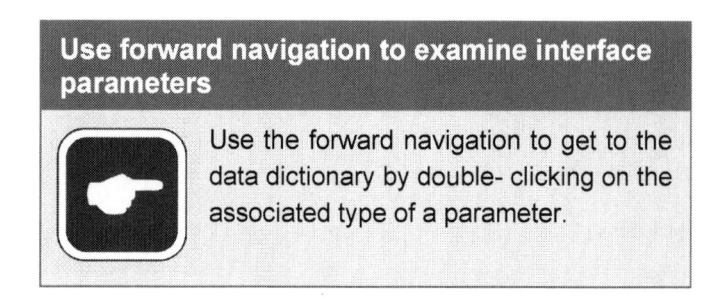

> **Use forward navigation to examine interface parameters**
>
> Use the forward navigation to get to the data dictionary by double- clicking on the associated type of a parameter.

The EXCEPTIONS tab shows predefined error cases foreseen by the developer of the function module. Using exceptions allows you to react to these error cases without the application stopping with a runtime error. Still, you will see in our first example, BAPI_FLIGHT_GETLIST, does not have any predefined exceptions.

Returning to our arithmetic example, let's now look at another function module: MINI_CALC. Please examine that function module; it is also part of the standard ABAP delivery. You will see that this function module is different than BAPI_FLIGHT_GETLIST: MINI_CALC is not remotely enabled, it does not reference DDIC objects for the interface parts, but it *does* use exceptions.

Assuming that the function module acts as a simple calculator, it seems appropriate to address the following error situations: division by zero, or use of a wrong operator. Indeed the function module notes these two error situations as exceptions, as displayed in Figure 5.6.

Function module	MINI_CALC	Active

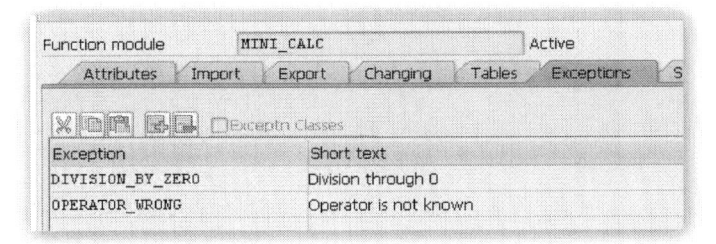

Attributes | Import | Export | Changing | Tables | Exceptions | S

Exception	Short text
DIVISION_BY_ZERO	Division through 0
OPERATOR_WRONG	Operator is not known

Figure 5.6: Function module MINI_CALC exceptions

Each exception is assigned a number, in order by its occurrence in the exception list, starting with 1. If during the call an exception is raised by the coding, this number is transferred into the system variable SY-SUBRC of the calling application. So SY-SUBRC will have to be checked, as will be shown in the following section.

5.2.3 Testing existing function modules

The function builder has a test environment if you would like to get a taste of function module behavior. Be aware that the phrase *test* does not mean *simulation*: the coding of the function module is executed.

You can start the test either from the initial screen, or from the function module display by using function key F8 (or the appropriate menu entry or button). The function builder will create a simple user interface to enter values for the parameters passed to the function module.

After maintaining values on the initial screen (not shown), execute the test (again with function key F8), and the result screen will display. It shows the import parameters, as well as the output of the function module: export parameters and tables (if part of the interface), see Figure 5.7.

```
Test Function Module: Result Screen

Test for function group     CALC
Function module             MINI_CALC
Uppercase/Lowercase    ☐

Runtime:        22.311 Microseconds
```

Import parameters	Value
OPERAND1	23
OPERAND2	42
OPERATOR	+

Export parameters	Value
RESULT	65

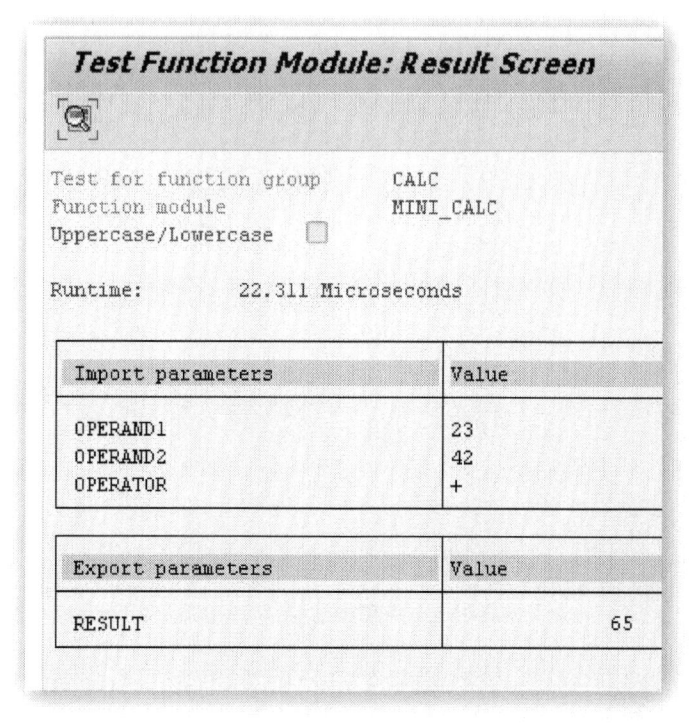

Figure 5.7: Testing a function module

Note that as MINI_CALC does not use any Tables parameter. And you may have to scroll horizontally to see the result parameter.

5.2.4 Calling existing function modules

When you want to call a function module, you should use pattern functionality in your report (offered as a button above the coding). It allows you to generate most of the CALL FUNCTION statement. Figure 5.8 shows the popup that appears when pressing the button PATTERN. When you specify the name of the function module and hit enter, the necessary CALL FUNCTION statement with all interface parameters of the function module are listed.

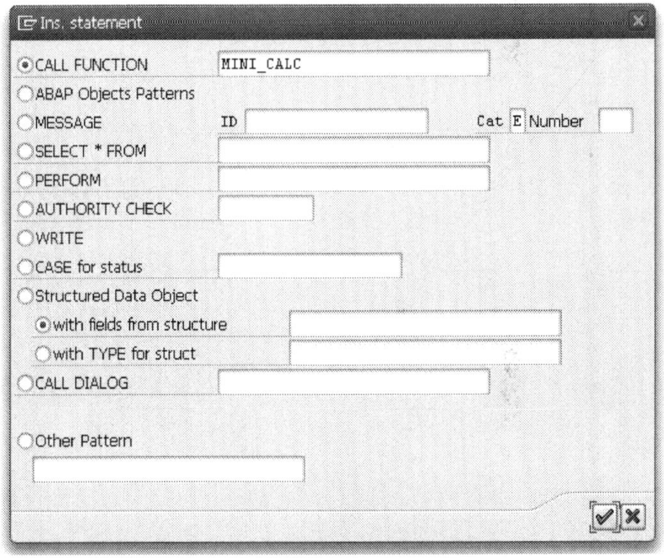

Figure 5.8: Pattern function for a function module call

You will have to pass local variables to the call and process the result, as well as react to error situations:

```
CALL FUNCTION 'MINI_CALC'
  EXPORTING
    operand1    = l_op1
    operand2    = l_op2
    operator    = l_oper
  IMPORTING
    RESULT      = l_res
  EXCEPTIONS
    DIVISION_BY_ZERO = 1
    OPERATOR_WRONG   = 2
    OTHERS      = 3
    .
IF sy-subrc <> 0.
* error handling
ENDIF.
```

Error handling can be improved using the case statement:

```
CASE sy-subrc.
  WHEN 0.
    WRITE: l_op1, ' ', l_oper, ' ', l_op2, '=', l_res.
  WHEN 1.
* error DIVISION_BY_ZERO was raised, react on it ...
  WHEN 2.
* error OPERATOR_WRONG was raised: react on it ...
  WHEN 3.
* unknown error occurred
ENDCASE.
```

Now, extend your report (with the form routine) using the function module instead of the form.

5.2.5 Understanding the importance of BAPIs

BAPIs are a subset of RFMs – what is so special about them? As they are presented as a business API, BAPIs offer a simple way to access (i.e. to read or to change) business data, based on an approach that seems object oriented (but only concerning the view of objects – the code itself is not object oriented).

BAPIs are essentially methods for business objects, like the method GETLIST for the object FLIGHT. This does not mean that the ABAP coding itself is object-oriented; as the BAPIs were introduced before ABAP became object-oriented (they are function modules). But the business data view and the search for a suitable BAPI to access the data are well structured.

Down the road, BAPI interfaces will not change, even with a new product release, but will be kept stable to prevent work for the applications calling the BAPI. When you compare the attributes of our two function modules examples, MINI_CALC and BAPI_FLIGHT_GETLIST, you will see that the BAPI function module is explicitly in status released, whereas MINI_CALC is not released. Each BAPI is released and well documented.

> **Exceptions not used in BAPIs**
>
> BAPI function modules always use a RETURN parameter to notify you whether or not any errors came up during the processing. RETURN can be a structure or an internal table, depending on the specific BAPI function module that is used.

And with their own transaction (named BAPI) to search for BAPIs and business objects, using it is even easier.

5.2.6 Case study: Reusing a BAPI in a report

Let's now create a report to display flight information using a function module. We will execute a call to the appropriate function module BAPI_FLIGHT_GETLIST to receive the flight information, and display parts of it on the list.

Step 1: Examine the interface.

To prepare, carefully examine the function module interface:

- ▶ Examine the Import parameters: DESTINATION_FROM and DESTINATION_TO are based on the DDIC structure BAPISFLDST. Both parameters need to be filled with a city and a country, respectively. We will need a complex data object (structure) for them in our report.

- ▶ Examine the Tables parameter: FLIGHT_LIST is based on the DDIC structure BAPISFLDAT, RETURN is based on BAPIRET2. We will need an internal table for both of them, as well as an associated structure as the work area.

Step 2: Test the function module.

As the next step in familiarizing yourself with the function module, you should test it to check which data will lead to which result. Note that this function module does not write any data on the database, so you may execute the test as often as you like without changing the database.

▶ Start the test environment from the display of the function module (Figure 5.4) using function key F8. The function builder displays the Import and Tables parameters. We only maintain the import parameters, shown in Figure 5.9:

Import parameters	Value
AIRLINE	
DESTINATION_FROM	🔲
DESTINATION_TO	🔲
MAX_ROWS	0

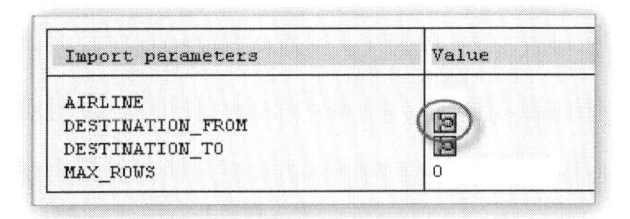

Figure 5.9: BAPI test import parameters

▶ Click on the structure icon next to DESTINATION_FROM (highlighted in Figure 5.9) to enter values for CITY and COUNTRY, as shown in the following Figure 5.10.

Structure Editor: Change DESTINATION_FROM

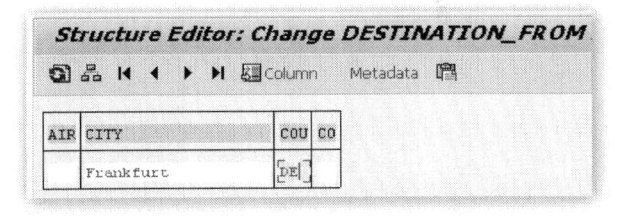

AIR	CITY	COU	CO
	Frankfurt	DE	

Figure 5.10: Structure editor for import parameter

▶ Repeat this for the second import parameter DESTINATION_TO with values "New York" and "US."

85

▶ Execute the test with function key F8. You will see the result. Click on the table icons (highlighted in Figure 5.11) to see the result details.

Import parameters	Value		
AIRLINE			
DESTINATION_FROM		FRANKFURT	DE
DESTINATION_TO		NEW YORK	US
MAX_ROWS	0		

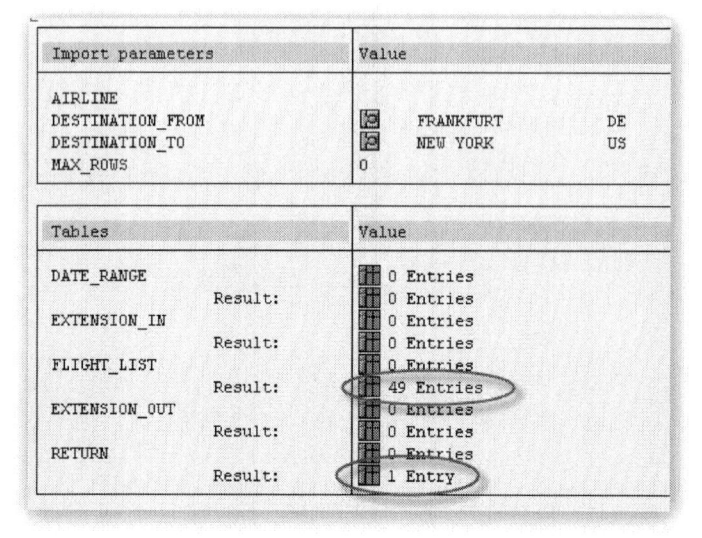

Tables	Value
DATE_RANGE	0 Entries
Result:	0 Entries
EXTENSION_IN	0 Entries
Result:	0 Entries
FLIGHT_LIST	0 Entries
Result:	49 Entries
EXTENSION_OUT	0 Entries
Result:	0 Entries
RETURN	0 Entries
Result:	1 Entry

Figure 5.11: BAPI test result

Repeat the test with values that are not valid, like 123 for city and country to induce error messages. Examine the contents of table RETURN, it contains more than one entry.

Step 3: Create the report and define the variables.

▶ Create a new report called z_display_flight_information.

```
REPORT z_display_flight_information.
```

▶ Define the variables: define four parameters for user input, referencing city and country fields of the DDIC structure BAPISFLDST.

```
PARAMETERS:
pa_frcit TYPE bapisfldst-city
         DEFAULT 'Frankfurt',
pa_frcnt TYPE bapisfldst-countr
         DEFAULT 'DE',
pa_tocit TYPE bapisfldst-city
         DEFAULT 'New York',
pa_tocnt TYPE bapisfldst-countr
         DEFAULT 'US'.
```

▶ Define two structures for the destination information, both based on the DDIC structure BAPISFLDST. These will be used in the function module call.

```
DATA: ls_dest_from TYPE bapisfldst,
      ls_dest_to   TYPE bapisfldst.
```

▶ Define an internal table for the flight data, and a work area, both referencing DDIC structure BAPISFLDAT. Define another internal table for the result information and a work area, both referencing BAPIRET2.

```
DATA: lt_flights  TYPE TABLE OF bapisfldat,
      wa_flight   TYPE bapisfldat,
      lt_rets     TYPE TABLE OF bapiret2,
      wa_ret      TYPE bapiret2.
```

▶ Pass the parameters filled by the user into the structures for the destination information.

```
ls_dest_from-city   = pa_frcit.
ls_dest_from-countr = pa_frcnt.
```

```
ls_dest_to-city     = pa_tocit.
ls_dest_to-countr   = pa_tocnt.
```

Step 4: Implement the call.

You will have to implement the call and provide variables for the interface parameters used (IMPORT and TABLES).

- ▶ Use the pattern function to get a skeleton for the call. Since exporting and tables parameters are optional, they are initially listed as a comment line. Note that your report *exports* parameters that are *imported* by the function module.

- ▶ Assign parameters and internal table to the call. Delete the comment sign for the appropriate lines (do not forget the lines with EXPORTING and TABLES). Keep the other lines in your coding for later use. Assign the respective local variables:

```
CALL FUNCTION 'BAPI_FLIGHT_GETLIST'
  EXPORTING
*   AIRLINE          =
    destination_from = ls_dest_from
    destination_to   = ls_dest_to
*   MAX_ROWS         =
  TABLES
*   DATE_RANGE       =
*   EXTENSION_IN     =
    flight_list      = lt_flights
*   EXTENSION_OUT    =
*   RETURN           =
    .
```

Now you may execute the report, but you will not be able see any results yet. You can use the debugger to examine the contents of the internal table. You should see the same number of entries as in your test. Note that you may even debug function module processing: set a breakpoint on the CALL FUNCTION statement, and step into it (F5).

Step 5: Display the result.

You will now use the work area for the internal table in the loop statement. Write selected fields of the structure to the list.

```
LOOP AT lt_flights INTO wa_flight.
  WRITE: / wa_flight-airlineid,
           wa_flight-airline,
           wa_flight-connectid,
           wa_flight-flightdate.
ENDLOOP.
```

Step 6: Check for error situations.

As the function module is a BAPI, it does not use exceptions. Instead the Table RETURN may contain information, so we will have to examine the contents of each line.

▶ Delete the comment from the line containing RETURN and assign your internal table.

```
...
return           = lt_rets.
```

▶ Loop over the table and write the content of the field MESSAGE.
Note that you may decide just to write error messages. For this, use the condition that field TYPE is not 'S' or blank (some BAPIs put 'S' for success in, some leave that field empty).

```
LOOP AT lt_rets INTO wa_ret
*  WHERE type NE 'S' OR type NE ''
 .
  WRITE: wa_ret-message.
ENDLOOP.
```

Finally, you can simplify the use of your report by assigning selection texts for your four parameters, as *departure city* is easier to understand than *pa_frcit*.

5.3 Using ABAP classes

5.3.1 ABAP classes with attributes and methods

Let's now take a look at *ABAP objects*. The concept of ABAP classes as object-oriented enhancement of ABAP was introduced after ABAP was already well known as language for business applications ("Advanced Business Application Programming": ABAP).

This section introduces ABAP classes and methods as a modern version of the reuse and modularization technique, which you can use even without deeper knowledge of object orientation.

In the event that you already have a general understanding of object-oriented development, you will have no problems using the same concepts in ABAP. Classes are essentially a blueprint for objects, and objects are a type of complex variables with coding. A class contains meta information, which is used when one object is created. Objects as instances of a class reflect real life objects in the business software. A flight connection between two cities is a general concept and can be modeled as a class. Flight connections between different cities are different instances of the same class.

Polymorphism and inheritance can be used in ABAP objects as well, but will not be part of this introduction.

The principle of encapsulation is also used for attributes and methods of ABAP classes. Attributes and methods can be private (accessible only from the class itself) or public (access is possible from the outside). The class can have instance or static methods: static methods can be called without instantiating the class (creating an object), in contrast to instance methods that are executed on a specific instance of the class.

An example for a static method for the class flight connection can be the method getFlightConnections, returning the list of all flight connections for a given selection. The method getFlightTime on the other hand, is instance-related since it would only return the flight duration for one specific flight connection.

Please note that an ABAP class and its methods cannot be executed remotely (from another system): the protocol RFC can only be used for RFMs. Still there are ways to expose an ABAP method for example as a Web Service, which is not discussed in this introduction.

The concept of ABAP classes and methods is an important one – not only concerning reuse and modularization. We will now jump into creating our own class and using it in a report afterwards.

5.3.2 Using the class builder to create an ABAP class

You can use the ABAP class builder (transaction SE24) to examine existing ABAP classes, or to create new classes. Of course, the class builder is integrated in the ABAP Workbench as well.

> **Local classes**
>
> Note that classes may be defined locally in your coding as well, but it is best practice to use the class builder to create a global class that is available for all applications.
>
> Do not mix that up with the meaning of local objects that are part of the package $TMP.

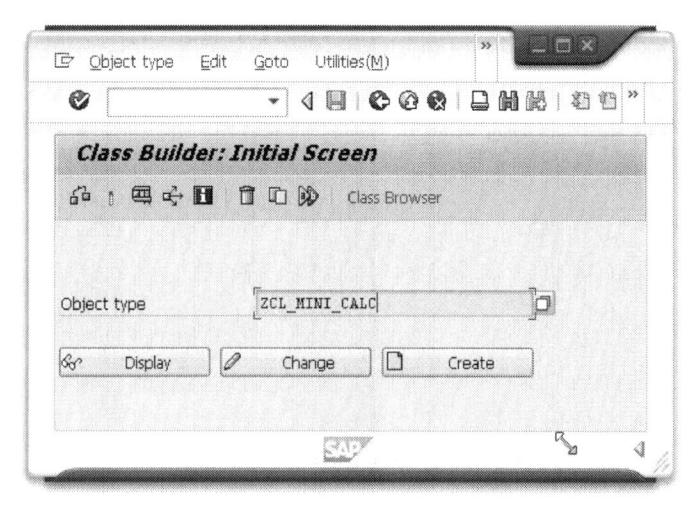

Figure 5.12: Initial class builder screen

On the initial screen (see Figure 5.12), enter the name of the class you want to create as ZCL_MINI_CALC and select the CREATE button.

On the following popup (not shown), you will enter a descriptive text for the class ("Provide calculation method") and keep all other parameters at their default values. After closing the first popup by clicking Enter, the next popup asks for an assignment of the class to a package. Save the class as a local object (i.e. into package $TMP). If you choose an existing package instead, you will have to specify the transport request as well, as discussed before.

Now the new class is displayed in the class builder and needs to be implemented. Several tabs are available; let's start with the METHODS tab that is initially displayed. Let's define a method CALCULATE: enter the method name, and use the input help for the level (static method) and visibility (public) of the class. Then enter a description, as shown in Figure 5.13.

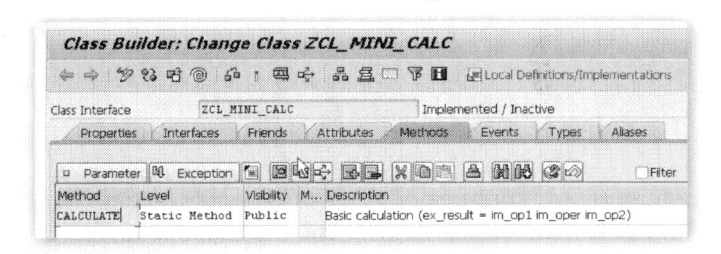

Figure 5.13: Create a method for the new class

Two further steps are now necessary: specify the method interface (list parameter names and types) and implement the method (insert coding).

Keep the line of your new method selected (click on any field in the first line), and use the button PARAMETER to switch to the maintenance of the method parameters.

Now enter four PARAMETER names, their TYPE (import or export) and their ASSOCIATED TYPE, as displayed in the following Figure 5.14.

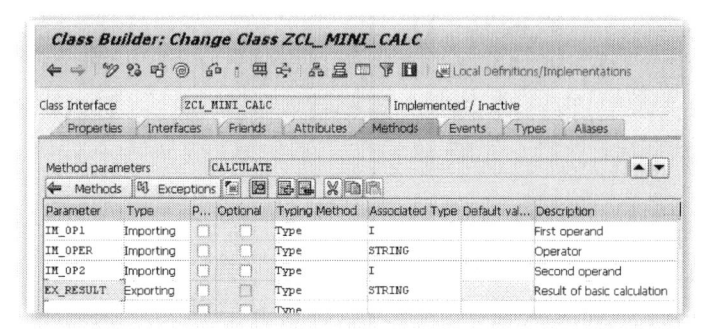

Parameter	Type	P...	Optional	Typing Method	Associated Type	Default val...	Description
IM_OP1	Importing	□	□	Type	I		First operand
IM_OPER	Importing	□	□	Type	STRING		Operator
IM_OP2	Importing	□	□	Type	I		Second operand
EX_RESULT	Exporting	□	□	Type	STRING		Result of basic calculation

Figure 5.14: Method parameters

The name prefix for import or export parameters is not necessary, but it may be helpful. The interface lists parameters for both directions (import and export) in one place. Only error situations (exceptions) are handled differently, which we will cover later.

Save the parameters and return to the initial display of your class by using the button METHODS (or function key F3).

To implement the method, double click on the method's name. The displayed view contains a section to implement the code, and the signature of the method can be displayed (or hidden) by using the button SIGNATURE as shown in Figure 5.15.

MODULARIZATION AND REUSING FUNCTIONALITY

> **Details on method parameter types**
>
> Apart from IMPORTING and EXPORTING, a parameter can be typed as CHANGING, which is both import and export.
>
> There is no special area for internal tables: a parameter just has to reference a *table type* from DDIC as associated type to be used for internal tables.
>
> And a parameter can be typed as RETURNING. This is only relevant for functional methods that return just one value, and which can be easily used as part of another ABAP statement.

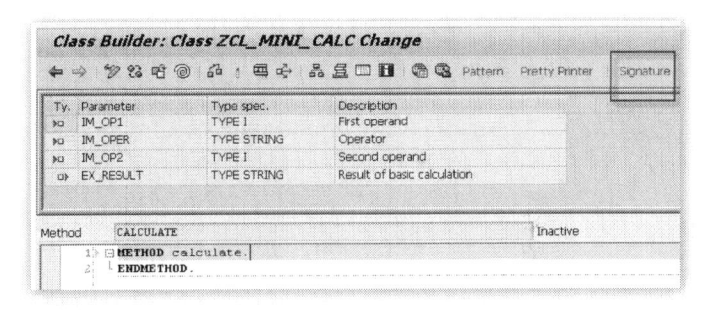

Figure 5.15: Method implementation with signature

For the implementation, we use code like before.

```
METHOD calculate.

  CASE im_oper.
    WHEN '+'.
      ex_result = im_op1 + im_op2.
    WHEN '-'.
```

95

```
        ex_result = im_op1 - im_op2.
      WHEN '*'.
        ex_result = im_op1 * im_op2.
      WHEN '/'.
        IF im_op2 = 0.
          ex_result = 'division by zero'.
        ELSE.
          ex_result = im_op1 / im_op2.
        ENDIF.
      WHEN OTHERS.
        ex_result = 'wrong operator'.
    ENDCASE.

ENDMETHOD.
```

Concerning the two error situations, let's start with hard coded strings that will be replaced by an exception concept in a later step.

Save and activate all of your objects. Your first ABAP class is ready to be used. Creating an instance method for the class works the same way, just set the level to instance instead of static.

You may check the object list for your class: it lists the method, and a double click on the methods name shows the coding.

5.3.3 Testing methods of an ABAP class

To test the static method of your class, choose the button Test/Execute (F8). This works if the details of your method are displayed. In case the entire class is displayed, you first have to select the method you are going to test (single click).

The class is listed with attributes and methods – in our simple case just one method, as listed in Figure 5.16.

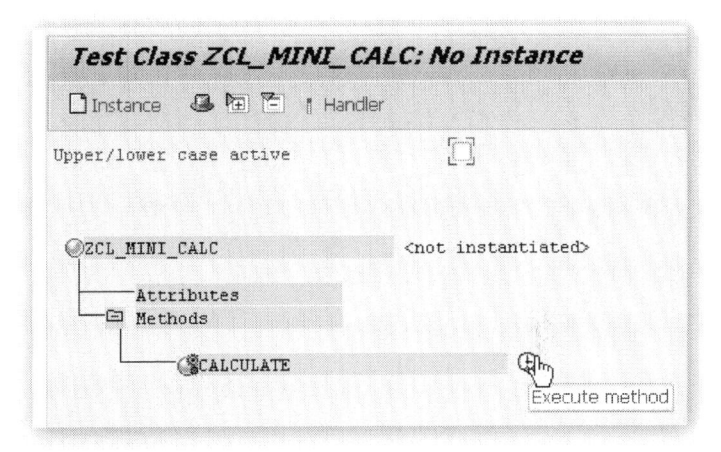

Figure 5.16: Starting the test for a class method

Choose the button next to the methods name to execute the method, as shown in Figure 5.16 above. A simple UI is generated, and you have to fill in values for the three input parameters (see Figure 5.17). For the operator, click on the icon to fill in the string value.

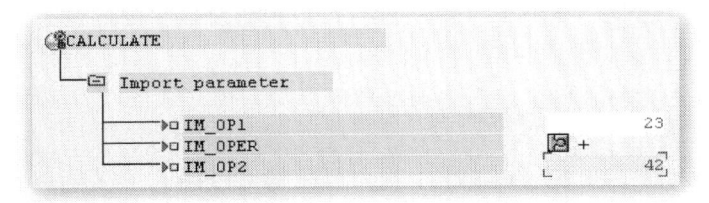

Figure 5.17: Specifying method test import parameters

Select the execute button again and the export parameter is listed as the result of the method execution (Figure 5.18).

```
CALCULATE
  Import parameter
    IM_OP1                          23
    IM_OPER                      + 
    IM_OP2                          42
  Export params
    EX_RESULT                       65
```

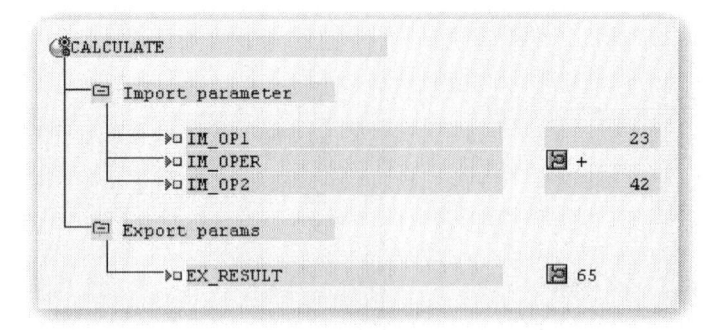

Figure 5.18: Class method test result

5.3.4 Calling class methods from your coding

How should you use class methods in your coding?

It is similar to the call of a function module: use the statement CALL METHOD (instead of CALL), and specify the class and the method (instead of the function module name), combined with a specific arrow (=>), and followed by the parameter assignments:

```
CALL METHOD zcl_mini_calc=>calculate
  EXPORTING
    im_op1  =
    im_oper =
    im_op2  =
* IMPORTING
*   ex_result =
  .
```

You can create this skeleton for the call by using the pattern function: choose ABAP Objects Pattern on the first popup (not shown), and specify the class and method name, as shown in Figure 5.19:

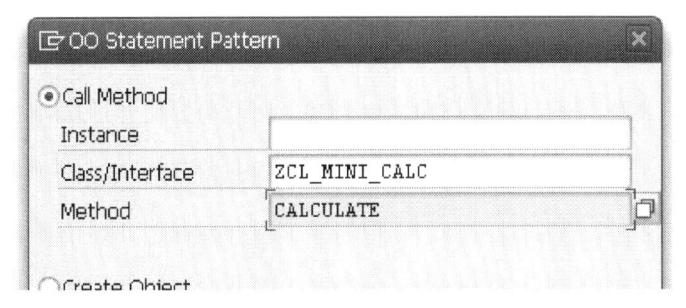

Figure 5.19: Pattern for class method call

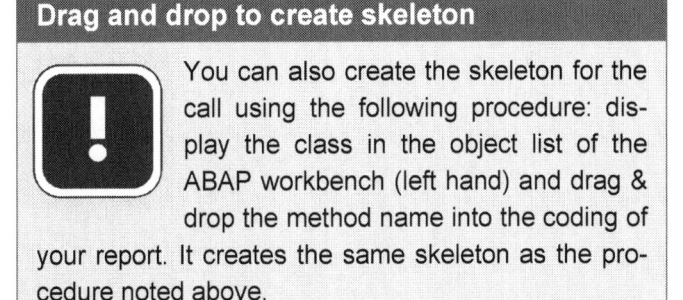

> ### Drag and drop to create skeleton
>
> You can also create the skeleton for the call using the following procedure: display the class in the object list of the ABAP workbench (left hand) and drag & drop the method name into the coding of your report. It creates the same skeleton as the procedure noted above.
>
> Drag and drop works for function modules as well: it creates the skeleton for the call of the module.

If the method was an instance method, the skeleton is similar (and can be created in the same way), but the sign between class and method is different (->). But we have to execute the method on an instance of the class, which has to be created first.

So first we need a data declaration for the object to be instantiated (DATA ... TYPE REF TO ...). Then we use this data object to instantiate the class (CREATE OBJECT...). And finally we specify the method name with a simple arrow (->) between the *object* name (instead of

99

the class name) and the method name. Let's put this into the context of the complete report:

```
REPORT z_mini_calc_on_class.

PARAMETERS: pa_op1 TYPE i, pa_oper TYPE string,
            pa_op2 TYPE i.

DATA: l_result TYPE string.

DATA: lo_calculator TYPE REF TO zcl_mini_calc.

CREATE OBJECT lo_calculator.

CALL METHOD lo_calculator->calculate
  EXPORTING
    im_op1   = pa_op1
    im_oper  = pa_oper
    im_op2   = pa_op2
  IMPORTING
    ex_result = l_result.

WRITE l_result.
```

Constructor method and create object statement

Classes can have a class-specific constructor (special named method CONSTRUCTOR of that class). If the class has a method with that name, the method is called implicitly when an object is created. If the constructor method has mandatory parameters, then these parameters have to be supplied with the CREATE OBJECT statement.

5.4 Exception concept for classes

The concept of exceptions for function modules has already been discussed. For ABAP classes, a different (and more modern) concept for exceptions is used which is based on exception classes (which is a class type).

You can use existing exception classes or create your own exception class for your purpose. All exception classes are derived from the exception class CX_ROOT (as super class) and its subclasses CX_NO_CHECK, CX_DYNAMIC_CHECK and CX_STATIC_CHECK.

> **Note on exception classes**
>
> An exception class needs another exception class as super class, for example CX_STATIC_CHECK (CX_ROOT is not possible). A super class is a class from which the class inherits characteristics, like attributes.

The exception concept for classes is based on the following parts:

1. Exception usage declaration
2. Exception usage
3. Exception handling

1) The declaration of the exception usage is relevant for a class method which intends to use an exception class in its implementation. Like with the parameters of a class method, you declare the exceptions for a method using a button in the class builder – as shown in Figure 5.13 where the method name was entered. Let's assume that

the method uses exception CX_SY_ZERODIVIDE, as demonstrated in Figure 5.20.

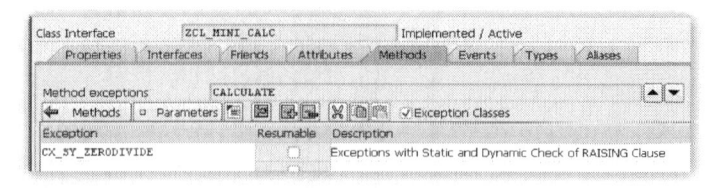

Figure 5.20: Exception usage for class method

2) The exception usage is part of the method implementation. For appropriate error situations, the method can use the exception with the statement RAISE EXCEPTION. The exception class has to be specified as TYPE. This is exemplarily used in the code of the method CALCULATE of the class ZCL_MINI_CALC:

```
    WHEN '/'.
      IF im_op2 = 0.
*     ex_result = 'divison by zero'.
         RAISE EXCEPTION TYPE cx_sy_zerodivide.
      ELSE.
         ex_result = im_op1 / im_op2.
      ENDIF.
    WHEN OTHERS.
```

3) The exception handling is part of the code that calls the class method and is based on a try/catch block:

```
TRY.
    CREATE OBJECT lo_calculator.

    CALL METHOD lo_calculator->calculate
      EXPORTING
```

```
        im_op1    = pa_op1
        im_op2    = pa_op2
        im_oper   = pa_op
      IMPORTING
        ex_result = l_result.
    WRITE: l_result.

  CATCH cx_sy_zerodivide.
    WRITE: 'error: division by zero'.
ENDTRY.
```

To analyze the exception, it is useful to create an exception object for the class and use one of the exception class methods to retrieve more information about the error situation.

The exception object first has to be declared:

```
DATA: lx_myexception TYPE REF TO cx_sy_zerodivide.
```

Then the catch block has to be extended to CATCH ... INTO:

```
CATCH cx_sy_zerodivide INTO lx_myexception.
```

Now the exception object is instantiated and holds attributes about the situation. These attributes cannot be read directly as they are encapsulated in the object, so we need to use a method instead:

```
l_text = lx_myexception->get_text( ).
WRITE l_text.
```

This presumes that l_text was previously declared as a string variable.

The try/catch block is relevant even for situations where the coding of the method does not explicitly use the RAISE EXCEPTION statement, but the exception is implicitly thrown by the system. Try this out by removing the handling of the division-by-zero case in the class method, as indicated here:

```
WHEN '/'.
    ex_result = im_op1 / im_op2.
WHEN OTHERS.
```

Although the exception is not thrown by your code in the method, it can be caught in your report.

6 Accessing the database

ABAP allows for the development of modern and efficient business applications to collect, store, and work on business data. The storage is a database, so we will examine the ways to access the database.

6.1 Using ABAP statements to access the database

6.1.1 Understanding the benefits of Open SQL statements

The ABAP system works with a relational database management system (RDBMS).

If you want to work with database tables in ABAP, you use *Open SQL* statements. That means that these statements are independent of the underlying database type (database vendor and operation system of the application server). This way, the ABAP applications using Open SQL statements can be used on all supported platforms without changes or adaptations. The database interface, which is part of the *work process* (the executable program that runs the ABAP report), takes care of the translation into *Native SQL*. This is shown in Figure 6.1 (which shows two of the three AS ABAP levels).

Before you start working with Open SQL statements, you should instead consider reusing existing functionality that simplifies database access. Look for appropriate existing function modules for BAPIs, or for methods of global classes. The advantage is that these will include additional mechanisms that are especially important for database changes (like executing authorization checks, following the locking concept, and considering the *update* mechanism in ABAP). As these advanced topics go beyond the scope of our ABAP introduction, the following sections will focus on read access only.

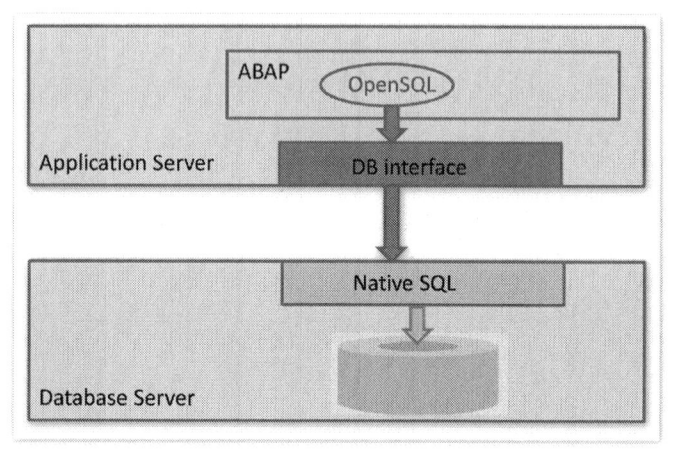

Figure 6.1: The database interface enables Open SQL in ABAP

Native SQL statements

It is also possible to execute Native SQL statements in ABAP. However, this is not recommended because it makes the ABAP coding dependent on the database type. The program will not always be able to be executed on systems with a different OS/DB combination.

6.1.2 Using Open SQL statements

The typical example to start with is the SELECT statement. It reads content (table fields) FROM the specified database table INTO a data object of the application (a structure or an internal table), taking a WHERE condition into account:

```
SELECT ... FROM ... INTO ... WHERE ...
```

To read all fields of a table entry, SELECT * is used (instead of specifying a selection of the table fields). Accordingly, the following examples read all fields from database table sflight into structure ls_flight or internal table lt_flights, which are defined as follows:

```
DATA: ls_flight TYPE sflight,
      lt_flights TYPE STANDARD TABLE OF sflight.
```

Note that for simplification, the examples below use hard coded values for the WHERE condition instead of variables.

1) Reading one line into a structure

Use the SELECT SINGLE statement to read a single record from the database into a structure:

```
SELECT SINGLE * FROM sflight INTO ls_flight
    WHERE carrid = 'LH' AND connid = '0400'
    AND fldate = '20131224'.
```

The where-condition has to be specific to one entry by using all key fields of the database table.

You should check the return value after the SELECT statement: SY-SUBRC has the value 0 if a suitable record was found.

2) Reading all entries into an internal table

Skip the addition SINGLE, and use the prefix TABLE for the target object (internal table) where the results will be copied:

```
SELECT * FROM sflight INTO TABLE lt_flights
    WHERE carrid = 'LH' AND connid = '0400'.
```

You should check the return value after the SELECT statement: SY-SUBRC has a value of 0 if at least one record was copied to the internal table. SY-DBCNT then contains the number of rows read.

3) Using SELECT as a loop copying entries into a structure

Assuming that several database table entries apply to the where-condition, you create a loop with the SELECT statement and copy one entry per loop pass into the structure ls_flight:

```
SELECT * FROM sflight INTO ls_flight
    WHERE carrid = 'LH' AND connid = '0400'.
    ...
ENDSELECT.
```

You should check the return value after the ENDSELECT statement: SY-SUBRC has a value of 0 if at least one row was read in the SELECT loop. SY-DBCNT then contains the number of records read.

For all three cases, the client field does not have to be specified because the current client is used by default. The addition CLIENT SPECIFIC allows you to specify a client different than the current one.

The following Figure 6.2 illustrates the three cases for the SELECT statement.

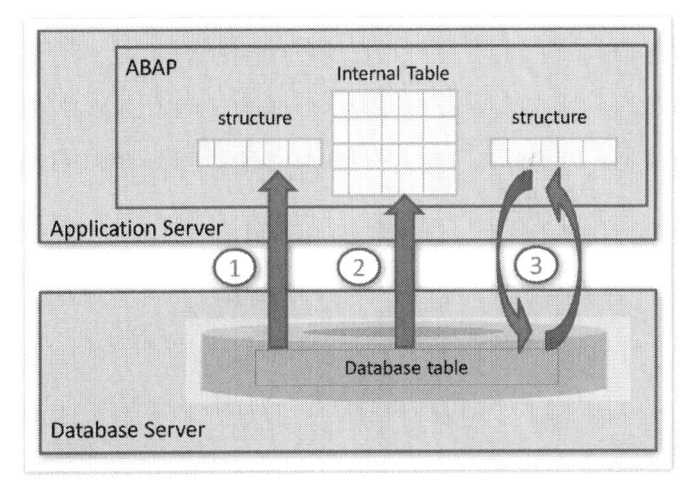

Figure 6.2: Using the SELECT statement to access the database

The third case in particular allows you to work directly on single table entries, for example to write the content to the list buffer. In the second case (SELECT ... INTO TABLE), an additional LOOP AT statement would be required to access single table entries. If, on the other hand, all entries should be stored in an internal table, the SELECT / ENDSELECT statement requires a dedicated statement in the loop to add the respective entry to the internal table.

In the following section, simple reports show this difference for the example of reading from database table sflight and displaying the results on a list. For the second case, a structure is used as a work area for the LOOP AT statement, as illustrated in Figure 6.3, because the WRITE statement can't access the entries in the internal table directly.

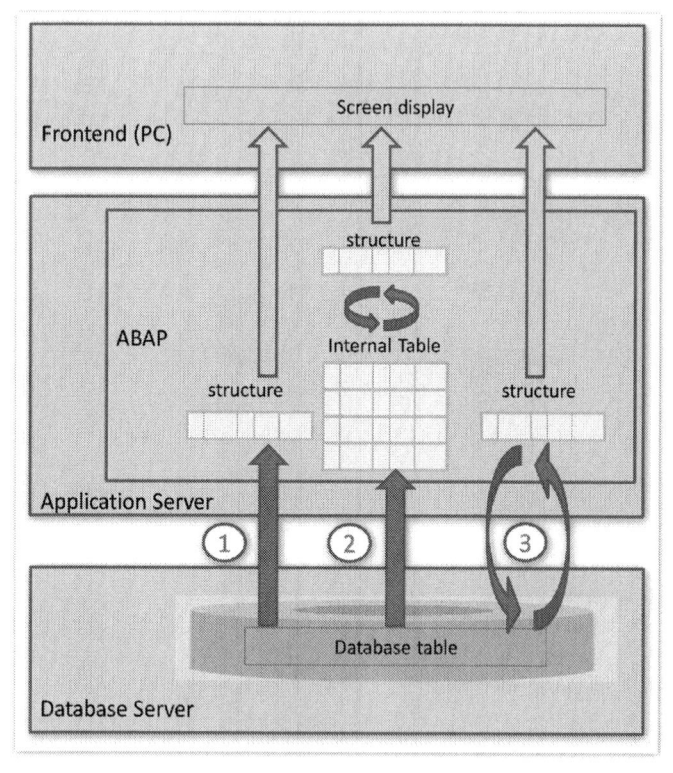

Figure 6.3: Displaying results of reading a database table

1) Reading one line into a structure

```
REPORT z_select_01 .

DATA: ls_flight TYPE sflight.
```

```
PARAMETERS:
pa_carid TYPE sflight-carrid DEFAULT 'LH',
pa_conid TYPE sflight-connid DEFAULT '0400',
pa_date  TYPE sflight-fldate DEFAULT '20130302'.

SELECT SINGLE * FROM sflight INTO ls_flight
   WHERE carrid = pa_carid AND connid = pa_conid
   AND fldate = pa_date.

IF sy-subrc NE 0.
  WRITE sy-subrc.
ELSE.
  WRITE: pa_carid, pa_conid, pa_date, /
  ls_flight-planetype, ls_flight-
  seatsmax, ls_flight-seatsocc.
ENDIF.
```

2) Reading all entries into an internal table

```
REPORT z_select_02 .

DATA: ls_flight TYPE sflight,
      lt_flights TYPE STANDARD TABLE OF sflight.

PARAMETERS:
pa_carid TYPE sflight-carrid DEFAULT 'LH',
pa_conid TYPE sflight-connid DEFAULT '0400'.

SELECT * FROM sflight INTO TABLE lt_flights
   WHERE carrid = pa_carid AND connid = pa_conid.

IF sy-subrc NE 0.
  WRITE sy-subrc.
```

```
ELSE.
  WRITE: pa_carid, pa_conid, sy-dbcnt.
  LOOP AT lt_flights INTO ls_flight.
    WRITE: / ls_flight-planetype, ls_flight-
    seatsmax, ls_flight-seatsocc.
  ENDLOOP.
ENDIF.
```

3) Using SELECT as a loop copying entries into a structure

```
REPORT z_select_03 .

DATA: ls_flight TYPE sflight,
      lt_flights TYPE STANDARD TABLE OF sflight.

PARAMETERS:
pa_carid TYPE sflight-carrid DEFAULT 'LH',
pa_conid TYPE sflight-connid DEFAULT '0400'.

WRITE: pa_carid, pa_conid.

SELECT * FROM sflight INTO ls_flight
  WHERE carrid = pa_carid AND connid = pa_conid.
  WRITE: / ls_flight-planetype, ls_flight-
  seatsmax, ls_flight-seatsocc.
ENDSELECT.
IF sy-subrc NE 0.
  WRITE sy-subrc.
ELSE.
  WRITE: / sy-dbcnt.
ENDIF.
```

Performance considerations

Typical business application database tables can easily have hundreds of thousands entries, instead of the few that table sflight has. This emphasizes the importance of performance considerations for database access statements.

It is best practice to shape the SELECT statement as specifically as possible to read only required table entries. If possible, all key fields of a table should be specified. For the same reason, I recommend specifying the fields to be read, instead of using SELECT *. Using the SELECT ... INTO TABLE ... (case 2) is more efficient in regards to database access than using SELECT / ENDSELECT.

Another aspect of performance is to check the parameters before using them in the SELECT statement: did the user enter empty values? If yes, it doesn't make sense to spend time accessing the database without receiving results.

Security considerations

Another important consideration before using the SELECT statement is whether we allow the current user to see the results. What if your SELECT statement works on business data instead of the flight model? Every user that is allowed to start reports may start your report, and see the result. (To restrict this, you can use the ABAP statement AUTHORITY CHECK.)

These aspects of performance and security are already taken into consideration in the existing SAP function modules coding and global classes.

When it comes to database changes, you have to pay attention to even more aspects, as mentioned above: locking database tables, the *update* process technique, and keeping the *Logical Unit of Work* (LUW).

So as stated before, the statements for database changes will not be described in this introduction, as careless usage may lead to an inconsistent state on the database. Instead, I recommend looking for existing code like function modules and global classes.

7 ABAP User Interface Technologies

After a discussion of how to access data stored in a database, we will now focus on the other part of application development: displaying data to the end user, called User Interface (UI) technology.

7.1 Working with messages

An easy way to provide information to the user is using the keyword MESSAGE. A message is a short one-line text displayed to the user of your application. It consists of a text and a message type, at least:

```
MESSAGE 'Database access successful.' TYPE 'I'.
```

Type "I" is an information text, which will display in a separate popup window, as shown in Figure 7.1.

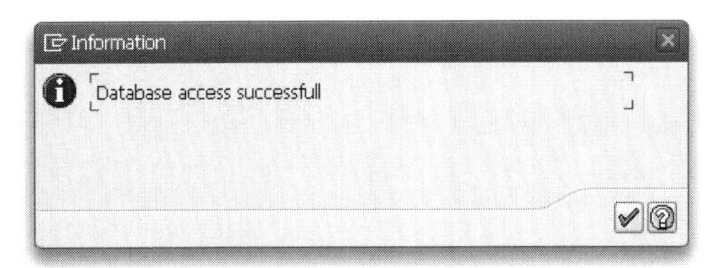

Figure 7.1: Message type I

Another message type is 'S' for success, which will show the message text in the status line of the following screen, see Figure 7.2.

☑ Database access successfull

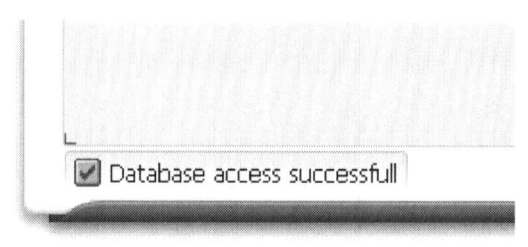

Figure 7.2: Message type S

It is not best practice to use hard coded text in your application, so all message texts should be stored in the database and referenced by a number instead. This way, the texts can be reused in other applications and can be translated.

Messages are stored in database table T100, grouped in message classes, and maintained with transaction SE91.

> **Message types use in DynPro applications**
>
> Additional message types ('W', 'E', 'A', 'X') are possible, but most relevant for DynPro applications. An introduction to DynPro applications will follow later, but without discussing messages.

For example, you may examine message class 00 (General Basis texts). Message 002 has the short text "Enter a valid value" that can be used during validation of user entries.

```
MESSAGE ID '00' TYPE 'I' NUMBER 002.
```

If you examine message 001, you will see that instead of readable text, it contains placeholders: a combination of a number and the ampersand sign like &1. These placeholders are used in message 006 and 007 as well. The variable text is specified using the "with" addition to the message statement:

```
MESSAGE ID '00' TYPE 'I' NUMBER 001
with 'Your user: ' sy-uname.
```

7.2 Working with list processing

As we have seen, a report is a good starting point for first steps in ABAP. For developing a new application reports are not the right choice; the ABAP programming guidelines categorize reports not used any longer. Still you have to have some knowledge of reports, especially when examining existing coding from SAP or from a former customer development project. And in some cases, it is faster and sufficient to create a report, for example for a short task or test. So let's look further at report details, most of them with regard to the user output, or user interface (UI).

7.2.1 Events in list processing

Let's start with a discussion of events which were already mentioned, but not used. Events are processing steps that occur at specific points in time during the processing of an application. Using them explicitly is optional as we have not used them yet, but it is best practice to do so.

The first event we will look at is INITIALIZATION, which occurs when the report is started and gives you the opportunity to initialize the selection screen input fields.

Next is AT SELECTION SCREEN which is processed directly before a selection screen is displayed to the user, and for some actions that the user of your report executed. The example report DEMO_SELECTION_SCREEN_EVENTS shows some examples for these actions.

The event START-OF-SELECTION is the standard processing block of an executable program (report). It is processed after any selection screens have been processed.

The last event introduced here is AT LINE-SELECTION which offers an easy way to react on user action on the list: it is triggered when the user of the report double-clicks on the list. For this, we have to explain the list concept of reports in more details.

As we have seen and discussed before, a report creates a list using the list buffer. You could say that a list is a screen only with text, without other screen elements. The text on the list is added to the list buffer using the WRITE statement.

Indeed a report can process multiple lists: a basic list and up to 20 detail lists. They all have an index starting with 0 for the basic list.

Now if the user of a report double-clicks a line of the basic list, the event AT LINE-SELECTION is triggered and the statements are executed that follow that event name:

```
REPORT  z_test_lists.
WRITE: 'basic list'.
AT LINE-SELECTION.
  WRITE 'next list'.
```

System variable sy-lsind is the list that is created, sy-listi is the index from which the event was triggered, and sy-lilli holds the number of the line that was double-clicked. Note that you can also set sy-lsind to determine which list to display next, and that even a double-click on a list that is not the basic list triggers the event AT LINE-SELECTION. Try this with the following simple example.

```
REPORT  z_list_buffer_demo.
WRITE: / 'basic list', / 'second line'.
AT LINE-SELECTION.
  WRITE: 'list level:', sy-lsind, / 'line clicked: ', sy-lilli.
  IF sy-lsind = 3.
    sy-lsind = 0.
  ENDIF.
```

You will see that the report title is displayed on the basic list, but not on the other list levels. So the first line that is written on the basic list equals line number 3 (variable sy-lilli).

7.2.2 Selection screens

The next step is to structure the selection screen which lists the parameters for the report. The statement SELECTION-SCREEN allows you to create a separate visual block with its own title:

```
SELECTION-SCREEN BEGIN OF BLOCK 0
  WITH FRAME TITLE text-001.
  PARAMETERS: pa_carid
    TYPE spfli-carrid DEFAULT 'LH'.
SELECTION-SCREEN END OF BLOCK 0.
```

Each block needs its own number. The title text-001 is a text symbol like used before.

Let's define a second block which contains radio-buttons for an easy choice, using the RADIOBUTTON addition:

```
SELECTION-SCREEN BEGIN OF BLOCK 1
  WITH FRAME TITLE text-002.
  PARAMETERS: p_sel RADIOBUTTON GROUP r1 ,
              p_fm RADIOBUTTON GROUP r1 .
SELECTION-SCREEN END OF BLOCK 1.
```

The GROUP specification is important to group radio-buttons, so that a selection is possible in each group only in case more than one group is used. Assuming that you have maintained selection texts for the parameters (including the radio-buttons) and texts for the selection screens, the selection screen should look like the one shown in Figure 7.3.

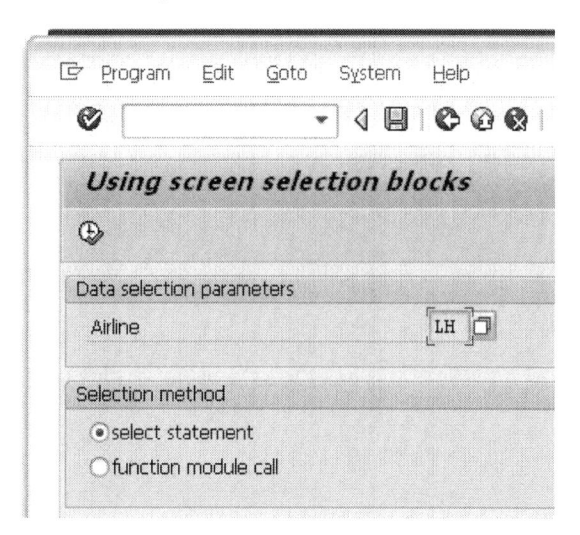

Figure 7.3: Using selection screen blocks

7.2.3 List formatting

You can format writing to the list several different ways. I'll cover some of them in the following section.

SKIP TO LINE ... allows writing to a specific line afterwards:

```
SKIP TO LINE 8.
WRITE: / 'This is line eight.'.
```

If you want the user of your report to double-click the list (to trigger the event AT LINE-SELECTION), it is helpful to emphasize this by using the HOTSPOT addition that will change the mouse pointer on the respective area.

```
WRITE: / '->', 'ALV display' HOTSPOT.
```

An even more prominent sign is to use an icon like ICON_LIST for a table, in this case combined with a HOTSPOT:

```
WRITE: / icon_list AS ICON HOTSPOT.
```

> **FORMAT statement**
>
> If you want to use these formatting options for more than one WRITE statement, use the FORMAT ... statement to define the formatting. After all WRITE statements are done, use the FORMAT ... OFF statement to reset the formatting.

To use a color, the addition COLOR followed by a color code can be used:

```
WRITE: / 'No result' COLOR COL_NEGATIVE.
```

The ABAP keyword documentation for FORMAT lists the possible color codes.

7.2.4 The ABAP list viewer (ALV)

If you want to display the content of an internal table, using the WRITE statement for all fields of a line is fussy. It is much easier to use the ABAP List Viewer (ALV) instead. The ALV offers a variety of possibilities and there are several ways to use it. The simple way is to call the function module REUSE_ALV_LIST_DISPLAY and pass the internal table along with the structure information to that function module:

```
CALL FUNCTION 'REUSE_ALV_LIST_DISPLAY'
EXPORTING
   i_structure_name = 'sflight'
TABLES
   t_outtab         = lt_flights.
```

7.2.5 Case study list processing

Let's put the features we just discussed into a simple example report that displays the existing flight data (from table sflight) for a given carrier ID. On the selection screen, the user can decide whether the report uses a SELECT statement, or simply calls a function module to read data from the database. If the selection has filled the internal table, the basic list will display the number of table entries and offers two ways to display the table content: simple list (using the WRITE statement) or the ABAP List Viewer (ALV).

We start with the event INITIALIZATION, containing the DATA declaration followed by two selection screen blocks discussed before. In addition, the event AT SELECTION-SCREEN is used to check whether the parameter pa_carid is initial.

```
REPORT  z_demo_list_processing.
INITIALIZATION.
DATA: l_lines TYPE i,
ls_flight TYPE sflight,
lt_flights TYPE STANDARD TABLE OF sflight,
ls_bapisfldat TYPE bapisfldat,
lt_bapisfldats TYPE STANDARD TABLE OF bapisfldat,
ls_ret TYPE bapiret2,
lt_rets TYPE STANDARD TABLE OF bapiret2.

SELECTION-SCREEN BEGIN OF BLOCK 0
 WITH FRAME TITLE text-001.
  PARAMETERS: pa_carid
    TYPE spfli-carrid DEFAULT 'LH'.
SELECTION-SCREEN END OF BLOCK 0.

SELECTION-SCREEN BEGIN OF BLOCK 1
 WITH FRAME TITLE text-002.
  PARAMETERS:  p_sel RADIOBUTTON GROUP r1 ,
               p_fm RADIOBUTTON GROUP r1 .
SELECTION-SCREEN END OF BLOCK 1.

AT SELECTION-SCREEN.
  IF pa_carid IS INITIAL.
    MESSAGE ID '00' TYPE 'E' NUMBER '001'
```

```
         WITH 'Specify carrier ID!'.
       EXIT.
     ENDIF.
```

The function module uses a different structure for the internal table (BAPISFLDAT) as the database table sflight, we need a separate combination of structure (ls_bapisfldat) and internal table (lt_bapisfldats). Note that the different structures will be relevant for the use of the ALV later as well.

After processing the selection screen, the event START-OF-SELECTION is triggered. Now we can use one of the radio-button parameters to distinguish between SELECT or CALL FUNCTION procedures. The variable l_lines is filled with the number of table entries. If the procedure did not read any data, this information will be written to the basic list (using red color). For the function module call, the RETURN parameter will be evaluated in addition.

The DESCRIBE statement is used to read the number of lines for the internal table for the CALL FUNCTION procedure.

```
START-OF-SELECTION.
  IF p_sel = 'X'.
    WRITE: 'Procedure SELECT statement'.
    SELECT * FROM sflight INTO TABLE lt_flights
        WHERE carrid = pa_carid .
    IF sy-subrc NE 0.
      WRITE: / 'No results for select.'
        COLOR COL_NEGATIVE.
```

```abap
    ENDIF.
    l_lines = sy-dbcnt.
  ELSE.
    WRITE: 'Procedure CALL FUNCTION'.
    CALL FUNCTION 'BAPI_FLIGHT_GETLIST'
      EXPORTING
        airline     = pa_carid
      TABLES
        flight_list = lt_bapisfldats
        return      = lt_rets.
    DESCRIBE TABLE lt_bapisfldats lines l_lines.
    IF l_lines = 0.
      WRITE: / 'No content in table'
        COLOR COL_NEGATIVE.
      LOOP AT lt_rets INTO ls_ret.
        WRITE ls_ret-message.
      ENDLOOP.
    ENDIF.
  ENDIF.
```

If the internal table doesn't have any entries, we exit the processing which shows the basic list with the message that no entries were found. Otherwise the basic list is enlarged, showing the two different lines for simple list processing or ALV usage (the latter with a HOTSPOT).

```abap
  IF l_lines = 0.
    EXIT.
  ELSE.
    WRITE: / 'Table with ', l_lines, 'lines.',
      /, '->', 'simple display' COLOR COL_NORMAL.
    SKIP TO LINE 8.
    WRITE: / '->', 'ALV display'
            COLOR COL_NORMAL HOTSPOT,
```

```
        icon_list AS ICON HOTSPOT.
ENDIF.
```

Finally the event AT LINE-SELECTION checks which line was selected. Either line 6 was double-clicked to get the simple list, or the HOTSPOT was selected on line 8 for the ALV usage.

As mentioned before, the ALV function module needs the structure of the internal table which differs for the two procedures. So we have to check the radio-button parameter p_sel again to know which structure to pass.

```
AT LINE-SELECTION.
  CASE sy-lilli.
    WHEN 6.
      IF p_sel = 'X'.
        LOOP AT lt_flights INTO ls_flight.
          WRITE: / ls_flight-carrid,
            ls_flight-connid, ls_flight-fldate.
        ENDLOOP.
      ELSE.
        LOOP AT lt_bapisfldats INTO ls_bapisfldat.
          WRITE: /
          ls_bapisfldat-airlineid,
          ls_bapisfldat-connectid,
          ls_bapisfldat-flightdate.
        ENDLOOP.
      ENDIF.
    WHEN 8.
      IF p_sel = 'X'.
        CALL FUNCTION 'REUSE_ALV_LIST_DISPLAY'
          EXPORTING
            i_structure_name = 'sflight'
```

```
          TABLES
            t_outtab         = lt_flights.
       ELSE.
         CALL FUNCTION 'REUSE_ALV_LIST_DISPLAY'
           EXPORTING
             i_structure_name = 'bapisfldat'
           TABLES
             t_outtab         = lt_bapisfldats.
       ENDIF.
    ENDCASE.
```

So the complete report is long and you should think about modularization so that you have clear and understandable code. The first step should be to create an include for the report and reference the include with the INCLUDE statement. This include could contain the DATA declarations. Forms could be defined in this include as well, so that the report flow is simplified. Operations like SELECT or CALL FUNCTION can be placed in methods in the include, so that the main report just contains the PERFORM statements for easier reading. But as forms are obsolete, you should rather think about creating a class with methods to modularize these tasks.

7.3 Working with screens and DynPros

The old-fashioned type of user interface technology in ABAP is DynPro technology, often referred to as screen processing. DynPro is an abbreviation of Dynamic Program. DynPros combine screens to display a user interface with modules that work on the data that are displayed to the end user (and the data entered by the end user). DynPro and screen are used as synonyms.

Nowadays more modern UI technologies are preferred over DynPros when you start developing a new application. Nevertheless, it is important to know the basics of DynPro technology to analyze existing applications because many SAP applications are based on DynPros.

A DynPro program is based on DynPros (screens) that are grouped in a screen sequence. The DynPros contain processing logic that determines the sequence, especially which screen to display next, and how to work with the data.

We started the ABAP introduction with *executable programs*, called reports. Reports can be started without a transaction code. DynPros are *module pool* programs and they do need a transaction code to be executed. That is why a *module pool* program is also called a *dialog transaction*.

DynPros can also be used in reports. This technique is relatively uncommon, but still a good starting point for us to learn the basics of screen processing.

7.3.1 Creating the first screen

Let's start fresh with a new report, so create a new report called Z_REPORT_WITH_SCREEN (without TOP include). The following Figure 7.4 shows the maintenance of the program attributes, in particular the program type MODULE POOL in the program type drop down menu. Remember that for screen processing (DynPros), typically a module pool is used, which is shown later. For our first example, keep the type to EXECUTABLE PROGRAM.

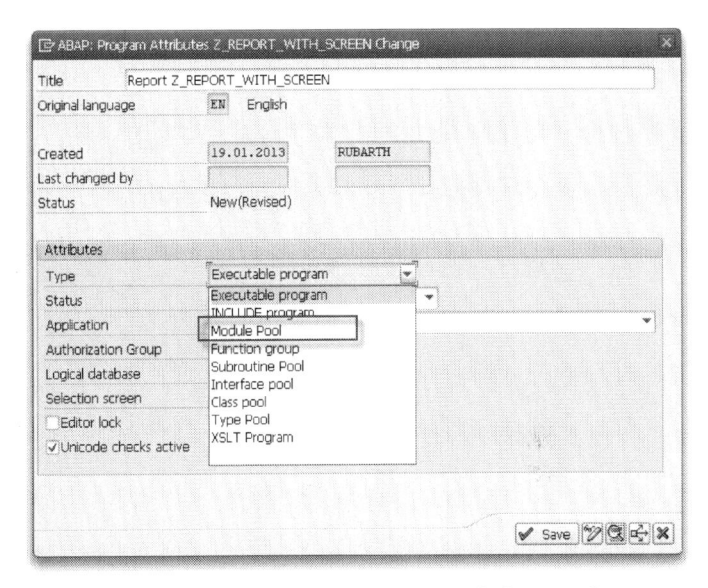

Figure 7.4: Program attribute maintenance during creation

After you have assigned the report to a package (like $TMP), you can start editing it.

It is easy to create the first screen: use the CALL SCREEN statement, followed by a screen number like 100:

```
CALL SCREEN 100.
```

Double-click on the number 100 to use the forward navigation. You will be asked whether you want to create the screen because it does not yet exist (popup not shown here). Choose yes, and the tool for screen maintenance opens: the screen painter. It creates the screen 100 for you and displays its attributes, as shown in Figure 7.5.

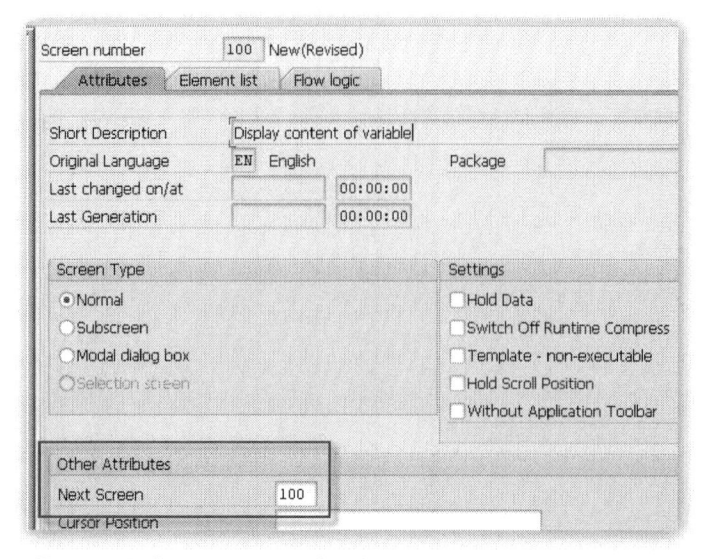

Figure 7.5: Screen painter showing screen attributes

Maintain a short description for the screen and keep all other attributes at their default values.

One attribute is important to mention here (and highlighted in Figure 7.5): NEXT SCREEN. In a screen sequence, you can set the value of the next screen that will be displayed after the current one here.

Of course the next screen to be displayed can be set dynamically during the processing of the screen. Remember that screens contain processing logic as well, apart from the UI elements.

The processing is defined on the tab FLOW LOGIC which lists modules to be executed. Initially, no modules are active as visible in Figure 7.6.

ABAP USER INTERFACE TECHNOLOGIES

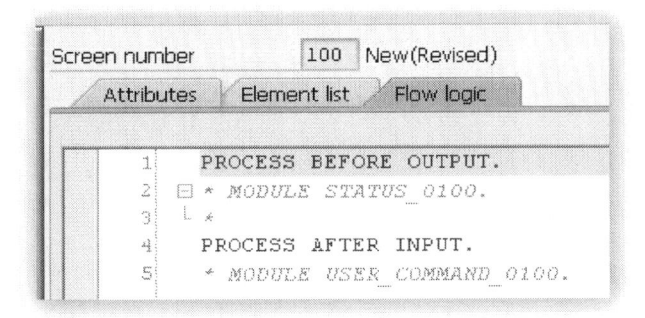

```
Screen number         100   New(Revised)
  Attributes    Element list    Flow logic

1   PROCESS BEFORE OUTPUT.
2   * MODULE STATUS 0100.
3   *
4   PROCESS AFTER INPUT.
5   * MODULE USER_COMMAND_0100.
```

Figure 7.6: Screen flow logic

The flow consists of two events: PROCESS BEFORE OUTPUT, (often referred to as PBO) and PROCESS AFTER INPUT (PAI). PBO lists all modules that are executed before the screen is displayed to the end user. PAI lists modules to be processed after the screen was displayed and a user action took place.

Flow Logic statements are not ABAP

The flow logic can have more statements than the simple list of modules, for example a loop. But these statements are not ABAP statements, although the editor looks like the ABAP editor. However, the statements *inside* the modules are ABAP statements.

Let's focus more on the UI elements you can enter using the tab ELEMENT LIST. The list is empty, and only allows you to edit one line. (The line has no name, but the type OK and we will discuss it later when the OK_CODE is introduced).

131

The reason is that another tool is responsible for adding elements to the screen: the Graphical Screen Painter. Click the button (LAYOUT to open this tool; it will open in a separate window, as shown in Figure 7.7.

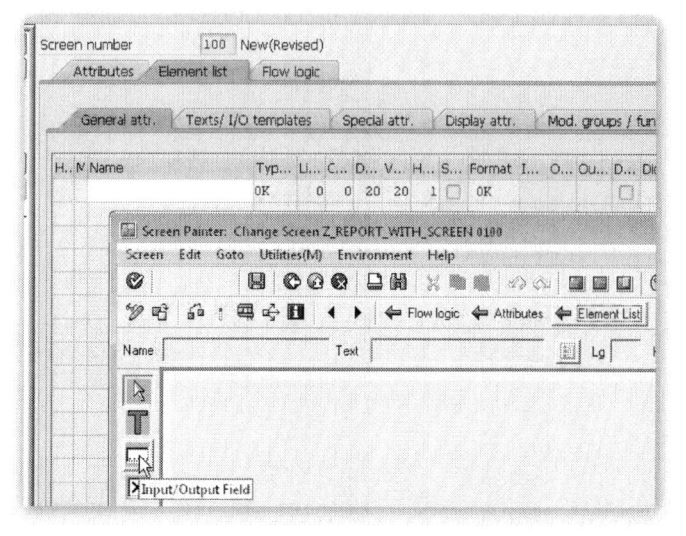

Figure 7.7: Graphical Screen Painter initial screen

The Graphical Screen Painter shows navigation buttons similar to the SAPGUI on top, and a selection of UI elements in the left hand area. Click the INPUT/OUTPUT FIELD button, as shown in Figure 7.7, and move the mouse over the grey background and then click on the background. An Input/Output field is created. Set the name to L_TEXT and the length to 30, as shown in Figure 7.8. (As long as you do not specify the name, the entry field for the name of the UI element is shown with a red background.)

ABAP USER INTERFACE TECHNOLOGIES

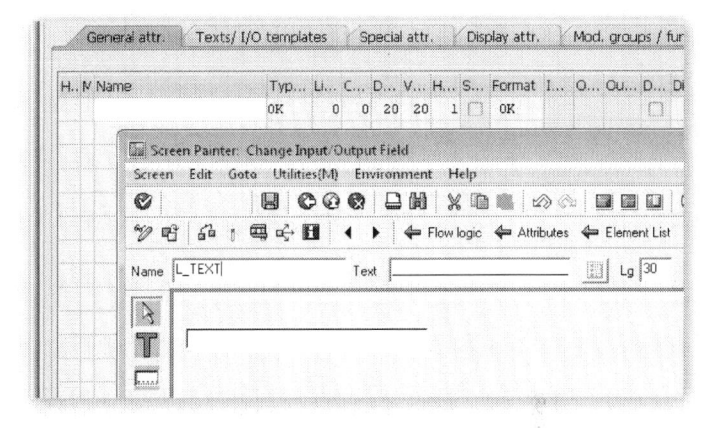

Figure 7.8: Graphical Screen Painter with one UI element

Save the change, and click the green back button (or F3) to return to the element list of screen 100 in the Screen Painter. After you return to the element list, the input/output field is added there.

When you use DynPros, it is important to remember that UI elements need a corresponding ABAP variable with exactly the same name. Create the corresponding variable (with default value) in your report before screen 100 is called and write the variable content to the list after the CALL SCREEN statement.

```
REPORT z_report_with_screen.

DATA: l_text(30) VALUE 'initial value'.

CALL SCREEN 100.

WRITE: l_text.
```

133

In this manner, a local variable is defined in the report and the content is transferred to the DynPro UI element which has the same name as the variable.

Still, we have to ensure that when the user clicks ENTER, the next screen will be set to 0 (instead of remaining 100, which means "no exit"). Click the tab Flow Logic and delete the preceding asterisk in the PAI area for the call of the module user_command_0100:

```
PROCESS AFTER INPUT.
  MODULE user_command_0100.
```

That means that this module will be processed after the user has entered a value (and pressed ENTER). Double-click the module name and confirm in the popup window that you want to create the module (not shown here). The following popup (see Figure 7.9) asks whether you want to create a new include for your report where the module will be placed, or whether the module will be placed inside the report.

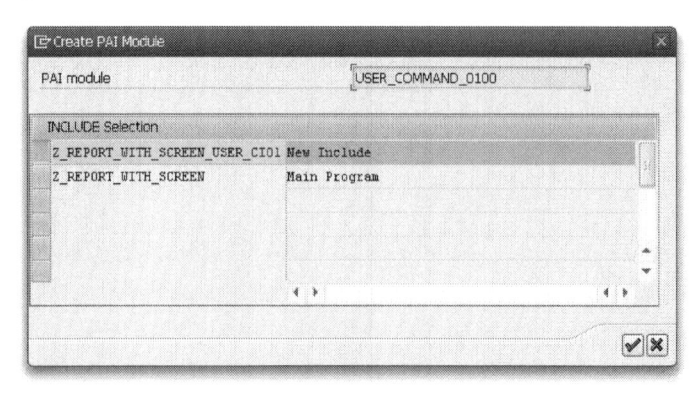

Figure 7.9: Create a PAI module for your report

Keep the suggested option to create a new include. The name is constructed from the name of the report, the name of the module, an "I" (for include) and a number, restricted by the maximum length of 30 characters.

The system will give you a warning message when the system adds an INCLUDE statement in your report, so that the include becomes part of your report. To confirm the message, click enter and the content of your include will be displayed.

Enter the statement to set the next screen to 0, which is equivalent to leaving the screen processing:

```
MODULE USER_COMMAND_0100 INPUT.
  SET SCREEN 0.
ENDMODULE.                " USER_COMMAND_01002 INPUT
```

The report object list (see Figure 7.10) shows all objects that are now part of it: the field, the module, the screen, and the include.

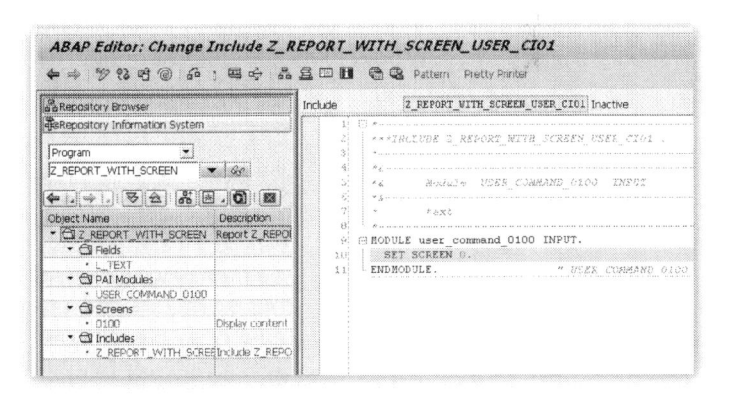

Figure 7.10: Object list of report with screen

Save the include.

You may adapt your report to have the INCLUDE statement right after the REPORT statement, but you do not have to.

Save and activate all objects. During activation the report, the include, and the DynPro will be listed as separate objects.

Currently the report just copies a value for a variable from the report to the screen and back to the report and finally gets written to the list.

Of course, we could have made this much easier by only using the PARAMETERS statement – but remember, we wanted a simple example for DynPro processing.

When you start the report, change the value of the UI element on screen 100 and press enter. The new value is transferred back from the UI element to the local variable and listed according to the WRITE statement.

Check the following: when a screen is displayed, you can use menu path SYSTEM/STATUS to validate which number the screen has, as this is listed in the popup under SAP DATA / REPOSITORY DATA.

Menus and buttons for DynPros

The menus System and Help are available by default. Other menus and buttons for actions can be defined using the tool Menu Painter which is not described in this introduction.

Identical names are relevant for a data transport between ABAP code and the screen. This is also the case when the content of a complete internal table is displayed (or even edited) on the screen. In this case, there are more conditions that should be considered. Still, a comprehensive explanation would go beyond the scope of this introduction.

As it may be helpful to understand the conditions for internal tables to analyze existing DynPro programs, in the next section we will cover how to use of a wizard to complete the necessary steps.

7.3.2 Using the table control wizard

The table control wizard helps you as a developer to meet all necessary conditions to show a table (in display or even in edit mode) to the user of the DynPro program. In the following section, we will first briefly discuss the use of the wizard and then we will look at a few examples of the results of the wizard's actions.

This time we will create a module pool program to see the differences to a report. Create a new program, name it SAPMZFLIGHTTABLE, keep the option WITH TOP INCL., as shown in Figure 7.11, and proceed by hitting ENTER.

Figure 7.11: Creating a module pool program

137

> **Different customer namespace for module pools**
>
> This name seems to violate the concept of customer namespace, which is not the case. In this specific case, the M is an indicator for a module pool and the Z afterwards is equivalent to the customer namespace.

On the next popup, the name MZFLIGHTTABLETOP will be suggested for the TOP include, confirm it by hitting enter. Note that TOP includes are used to define variables.

The following popup is the maintenance of the program attributes (compare with Figure 7.4). Keep the TYPE to module pool and proceed with SAVE. Assign a package (like $TMP), and finally the code for your program is displayed.

For a module pool, we do not explicitly add the statement CALL SCREEN 100. Instead, we create a screen using the context menu (right mouse click) for the program SAPMZFLIGHTTABLE in the object list, and specify the screen number as 100. (Later, we will create a transaction code with a reference to screen 100, which is the trigger to call that screen.)

Add a short description for the screen and save it. Click the (LAYOUT button to open the Graphical Screen Painter.

Now use the button TABLE CONTROL (WITH WIZARD) (third one from bottom) to create a UI element. This will open the Table Control wizard in a popup window.

After reading the introduction, click CONTINUE to proceed.

A table control has to be created. Since you started the wizard from within screen 100 of your report, the values for report and screen are already maintained. Specify the name of the control object as FLIGHTCONTROL and click CONTINUE to proceed.

Enter SPFLI as a table to be used from the data dictionary and click CONTINUE to proceed.

Select the lines for a selection of table fields, for example CARRID CONNID COUNTRYFR CITYFROM COUNTRYTO CITYTO. Click CONTINUE to proceed.

For the table control attributes, keep OUTPUT ONLY selected. Click CONTINUE to proceed.

Select the checkbox SCROLL to display scroll buttons for the table. Click CONTINUE to proceed.

Keep all proposed values for the includes and click CONTINUE to proceed.

Read the summary, then click FINISH to close the popup and return to the Graphical Screen Painter. You may have to resize the table control on the screen to see all of the columns.

Save the screen and return to the FLOW LOGIC.

Activate all objects: the program, the screen 100, and four includes. Apart from the TOP include, includes for the input (PBO) and for the output (PAI) modules are each created. In addition, the wizard creates a module with subroutines for the table control.

Use the context menu on the program and choose CRE-
ATE • TRANSACTION to create a transaction code for your
report. Name it ZTABCONTR, enter a short description
(like "table control test"), keep the START OBJECT selection to PROGRAM AND SCREEN, and confirm by clicking
ENTER. Finally, you have to maintain the program name
(can be copied from the object list) and screen number
which the transaction code will start. You should also
select the GUI SUPPORT parameter SAPGUI FOR WIN-
DOWS, as visible in Figure 7.12. After you have saved the
transaction code, you can either start it directly from the
display with the button TEST (F8), or by manually enter
the transaction code into the command field.

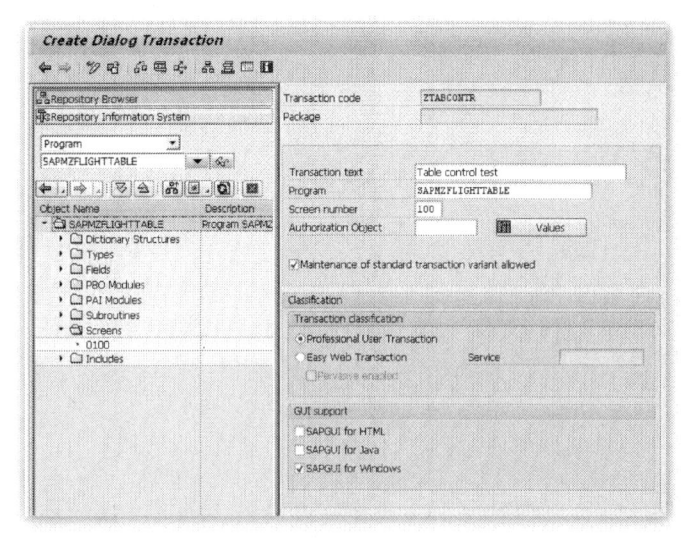

Figure 7.12: Create dialog transaction

You can now see the table content displayed in the table
control on screen 100. Use the scroll buttons to scroll
down and then up.

When you come to the point of wondering how to exit the program, remember that the NEXT SCREEN attribute of screen 100 is set to 100 and is not overwritten by any statement. Enter /nSE80 into the command field to leave the program and return to the ABAP Workbench.

If you want to solve this, don't set the next screen to 0 – neither change the NEXT SCREEN attribute of screen 100, nor use the statement SET SCREEN 100. These will both end your program each time you use a scroll button. Instead, we will introduce the concept of the OK_CODE as a variable containing the user actions.

Investigate the TOP include: among other declarations created by the wizard (discussed later) it contains a declaration for a variable called OK_CODE on the last line. For screen 100, this variable needs a UI element with identical name. Open the screen 100 element list and you will find the line for the OK_CODE: it is of type OK. In Figure 7.13, the line is highlighted (and some table lines are cut to simplify the image).

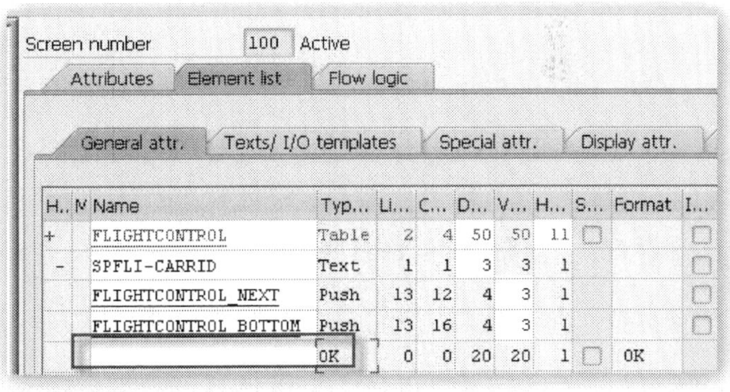

H..	N Name	Typ...	Li...	C...	D...	V...	H...	S...	Format	I...
+	FLIGHTCONTROL	Table	2	4	50	50	11			
-	SPFLI-CARRID	Text	1	1	3	3	1			
	FLIGHTCONTROL_NEXT	Push	13	12	4	3	1			
	FLIGHTCONTROL_BOTTOM	Push	13	16	4	3	1			
		OK	0	0	20	20	1		OK	

Figure 7.13: OK_CODE as screen UI element

Enter OK_CODE in the NAME field, and save the change.

By checking the value of OK_CODE, we have a way to check which action the end user did. Using a scroll button is an action that is associated with an OK_CODE value. (This association was set by the wizard as well). But entering a value into the command field is another way to set the value for OK_CODE.

Navigate to the Flow Control of screen 100 and examine the event PROCESS AFTER INPUT: after a loop (necessary for the table control), the module FLIGHTCONTROL_USER_COMMAND is called. Double-click the name of the module to navigate to it.

In the module, the wizard entered code. We can simply add three lines to the beginning of the module to check whether the end user has entered the value 'END' into the command field. If that is the case, we set the (next) screen to 0 to end the program:

```
MODULE flightcontrol_user_command INPUT.
  IF ok_code = 'END'.
    SET SCREEN 0.
  ENDIF.
  ok_code = sy-ucomm.
```

Save the change and execute the transaction code again. Navigate in the table to check that the scroll buttons do not end the program. Enter 'END' into the command field (without the preceding /n!) to see that the program is stopped. You can also set a breakpoint in the module to check the value of OK_CODE, for example when a scroll button is used.

> ### Command field is workaround
>
> As stated in a previous note, you typically use the menu painter to create buttons and menu entries to allow the end user to end the program without using the command field. These buttons and menus are associated with OK_CODE values as well.

Let's now look at some other parts of the generated code in the module pool. In the TOP include, DATA and TYPES statement are inserted and a CONTROL statement defines the control object that is associated with the table control UI element. The first statement is the TABLE statement for SPFLI, which defines a structure with the fields of the database table SPFLI.

> ### TABLE statement for structures
>
> One of the (still existing) mysteries of ABAP is the TABLE statement. It defines a *structure*, **not** an internal table! So the TABLE statement seems fully equivalent to the statement DATA <struct> TYPE <struct> (which we already used). But for programs using Dynpros, only the TABLE statement can be used to have a structure with field names identical to the UI elements on the screen.

The internal table into which the data from database table SPFLI are copied is defined as G_FLIGHTCONTROL_ITAB, and the associated work area structure is defined as G_FLIGHTCONTROL_WA.

Examine the event PROCESS_BEFORE_OUTPUT in the Flow Control of screen 100. A module FLIGHTCONTROL_INIT is called, which contains the SELECT statement to fill the internal table G_FLIGHTCONTROL_ITAB. This is only necessary once when the program is started, so the flag G_FLIGHTCONTROL_COPIED is set to true after the internal table is filled and the flag is checked before the SELECT statement.

You may examine other parts of the generated code. We conclude our journey into DynPro technology here after an introduction to screens, flow control, PBO and PAI modules, variables with identical names to UI elements, and the OK_CODE to check user actions.

7.4 Short overview on SAP UI technologies

As I mentioned, DynPro technology is rather old fashioned and the question is which other technology should be used nowadays. In contrast to the ABAP fundamentals we discussed that are more or less stable over the years, UI technologies have a fast innovation cycle and change rather quickly. This makes it difficult to discuss these technologies in this introduction because there is a risk that the information will be outdated after a few months.

Still some general differences are important to know, so let's take a quick look at the development of UI technology for ABAP.

7.4.1 Internet Transaction Server (ITS)

As the DynPro technology is bound to the SAPGUI to display the UI, the Internet Transaction Server (ITS) was introduced which converts DynPros into HTML pages in a generic way.

The ITS initially required a separate installation, but it is now part of the standard installation of AS ABAP. It presumes that your AS ABAP HTTP services are activated. You can start your transaction from a browser window by providing the transaction code, the client, and optionally the language via parameters the following way:

http://<host>:<port>/sap/bc/gui/sap/its/webgui?~transaction=ZTABCONTR&sap-client=001&sap-language=EN

Note the tilde before the transaction parameter.

But as the ITS converts all SAPGUI transactions, you can easily log on to your AS ABAP using the ITS, without any need for a local SAPGUI installation using the transaction webgui:

http://<host>:<port>/sap/bc/gui/sap/its/webgui?sap-client=001&sap-language=EN

As the ITS is a layer for conversion of DynPros to HTML, it does not offer a different approach to develop applications. (Initially the ITS had its own capability to develop web applications, but this technique is outdated).

7.4.2 Business Server Page (BSP) Applications

Instead of converting existing "classical" applications to HTML, Business Server Page Applications are already developed using HTML. Just like Java Server Pages (JSP) or Active Server Pages (ASP), the concept of Business Server Pages is to have static HTML and include dynamic parts that are executed when the page is requested from the browser processed by the server.

On a BSP page, the dynamic statements are encapsulated in specific tags starting with <% and ending with %>. The runtime of AS ABAP will interpret the content in-between as ABAP statements and process these. This type of static and dynamic content mix can be as simple as the following example:

```
<%@page language="abap" %>
<html><body><center>
<%
  do 5 times.
%>
<font size=<%= sy-index%>>
Hello World!<br />
</font>
<%
  enddo.
%>
</center></body></html>
```

To harmonize the UI and to ease the development of BSP applications, SAP introduced several sets of BSP-extensions (libraries) including HTMLB for HTML-Business, and other. If you create a BSP application (as a container) and an associated BSP page, a BSP-extension is used to set up the default content. Like with the screen sequence for DynPros, BSP pages have a sequence and a way to pass parameters and store data.

In this context, the Web Client UI framework has to be mentioned, since it is a technology that is based on BSP applications. The technique was first used in SAP Customer Relationship Management (SAP CRM) and can be used with AS ABAP as well. It is based on the Model View Controller (MVC) paradigm and was introduced shortly before Web Dynpro ABAP.

7.4.3 Web Dynpro ABAP

With the concept of Web Dynpro technology, SAP introduced a development approach for web applications nearly simultaneously for AS ABAP (Web Dynpro ABAP) and the SAP NetWeaver Application Server Java (Web Dynpro Java). The concept follows the Model View Controller (MVC) paradigm which is based on a framework. The developer defines the UI elements with position on the UI and where they get their data from, and the framework generates the code from these declarations. The advantage is that the development is independent from the frontend device because the framework generates the output dynamically based on the connected frontend.

Although the name Web Dynpro ABAP suggests a concept similar to DynPro technology (or even a way to convert DynPro to Web Dynpro), the two technologies do not have similarities and no conversion possibility exists.

Together with Web Dynpro ABAP, the "Floorplan Manager" (FPM) is a framework that provides a consistent look and feel. The Floorplan Manager is a set of tools, templates and classes and allows Web Dynpro ABAP application users a modification-free way of adapting existing UIs. Most application developments in the SAP Business Suite development are using this paradigm.

7.4.4 SAPUI5

SAPUI5 is a UI technology that is based on HTML5 standards. It supports mobile devices, as well major desktop browsers. SAPUI5 comes with a variety of UI controls and it can be extended by customer code or by other UI control libraries. It uses the javascript library jQuery and creates user interfaces that can connect to an AS ABAP backend with a variety of state of the art protocols like Web Services, RESTful services, and others. This decouples the UI technology from the application, and allows a flexible and up-to-date user experience.

> **SAPUI5 library available**
>
> Customers and partners can use the SAPUI5 library as well for their own applications, as it is available for download in the SAP Collaboration Network (SCN), *www.scn.sap.com*.

7.4.5 ABAP Development tools

When discussing user interface technologies, the user in focus was the end user that is using the application that we developed. But as a developer, you are a user as well because you are using the ABAP tools.

A new approach for ABAP development is using the Eclipse workbench as frontend development tool for ABAP. This even allows connecting to several ABAP backends at one time in one development environment. This rather new technique is officially called "ABAP Development Tools". In some cases, you may still read the former name "ABAP in eclipse". Although not all features are currently available, more and more features of the ABAP Workbench will be made available in eclipse.

8 Conclusion

We have covered the foundation of ABAP from the first "Hello world" example to modularization techniques and wrapped up with a look at UI technologies. You have now the necessary skillset to focus on your next steps. These can be related to UI technologies in detail, to interface technologies like Remote-Function-Call or Web Service integration, or to application development with storing data on the database.

espresso tutorials

You have finished the book.

Did you like what you read?

Then please write a review for this book!

Sign up for our newsletter!

Learn more about new e-books?

Get exclusive free downloads.

Sign up for our newsletter!

Please visit us on *newsletter.espresso-tutorials.com* to find out more.

A The Author

Dr. Boris Rubarth has more than 14 years of experience with SAP software. He started as an ABAP instructor for customer trainings at SAP Germany. Subsequently, he specialized on connectivity and integration topics and was responsible for creating a series of SAP training curricula. Boris now works as a Product Manager at SAP AG and lectures at various colleges on ABAP, SAP basis technology, and SAP NetWeaver Process Integration. He studied Physics in Hamburg and Hanover, and received his PhD in Physics in Oldenburg.

B Disclaimer

This publication contains references to the products of SAP AG.

SAP, R/3, SAP NetWeaver, Duet, PartnerEdge, ByDesign, SAP BusinessObjects Explorer, StreamWork, and other SAP products and services mentioned herein as well as their respective logos are trademarks or registered trademarks of SAP AG in Germany and other countries.

Business Objects and the Business Objects logo, BusinessObjects, Crystal Reports, Crystal Decisions, Web Intelligence, Xcelsius, and other Business Objects products and services mentioned herein as well as their respective logos are trademarks or registered trademarks of Business Objects Software Ltd. Business Objects is an SAP company.

Sybase and Adaptive Server, iAnywhere, Sybase 365, SQL Anywhere, and other Sybase products and services mentioned herein as well as their respective logos are trademarks or registered trademarks of Sybase, Inc. Sybase is an SAP company.

SAP AG is neither the author nor the publisher of this publication and is not responsible for its content. SAP Group shall not be liable for errors or omissions with respect to the materials. The only warranties for SAP Group products and services are those that are set forth in the express warranty statements accompanying such products and services, if any. Nothing herein should be construed as constituting an additional warranty.

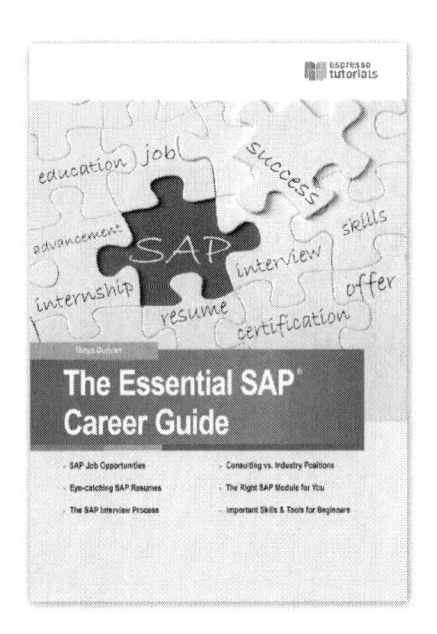

Tanya Duncan
The Essential SAP® Career Guide

A beginner's guide to SAP careers for students and professionals

SAP is the world's leading enterprise applications provider with software solutions for companies of all sizes and industries. Nearly 80% of Fortune 500 companies rely on SAP to run their inventory management, financials, human resources, purchasing, and sales business processes. There are numerous job opportunities for all experience levels and the right approach can fast-track your career. This book is written specifically for students and professionals aspiring to start a career with SAP as a consultant or user.

We'll cover key topics including:

- How to find a job with SAP
- Creating a stand-out SAP resume
- Preparing for your first SAP interview
- Opportunities for industry networking and involvement in SAP groups
- Choosing the right SAP module and how to develop skills in other modules
- Important skills and concepts to focus on when starting your career

This book is an extremely valuable resource for many young professionals starting their career in SAP and answers frequently asked questions.

Martin Munzel & Jörg Siebert
First Steps in SAP®

- ▶ Learn what SAP and SAP software is all about!
- ▶ Enhanced with videos and audio comments
- ▶ Simple, consecutive examples

If you would like to understand the basic fundamentals of SAP software without having to work through 300 pages or more, this book is for you! The authors concentrate on the essentials and spare you all the details you will not need as a beginner. Martin Munzel and Joerg Siebert can look back at a total of 25 years of experience with SAP software, and in this book, they share their profound knowledge in a precise, comprehensible manner. Using simple, consecutive examples, they take you through the basics you need to know about SAP:

- Navigating SAP ERP
- Transactions
- Organizational Units
- Master Data
- Process Design

The videos will help you experience the look-and-feel of SAP software without actually having access to an SAP system.

Ingo Brenckmann & Mathias Pöhling:
The SAP® HANA Project Guide

SAP HANA is the SAP product for in-memory computing. It streamlines transactions, analytics, planning, and data processing on a single in-memory database allowing businesses to operate in real-time. Over the course of the last few years, the authors have led many diverse SAP HANA projects with extraordinary success resulting in 10,000, or in some cases even 100,000, times improvement of system performance.

In this book, the authors share their findings from SAP HANA projects to help ensure the success of your SAP HANA project. The SAP HANA project guide will also help you identify suitable scenarios for your company to get started with in-memory computing, while sketching out a long term plan to provide innovation to your entire business using SAP HANA.

We'll cover the following key topics:

- Delivering innovation with SAP HANA
- Creating a business case for SAP HANA
- Thinking in-memory
- Managing SAP HANA projects

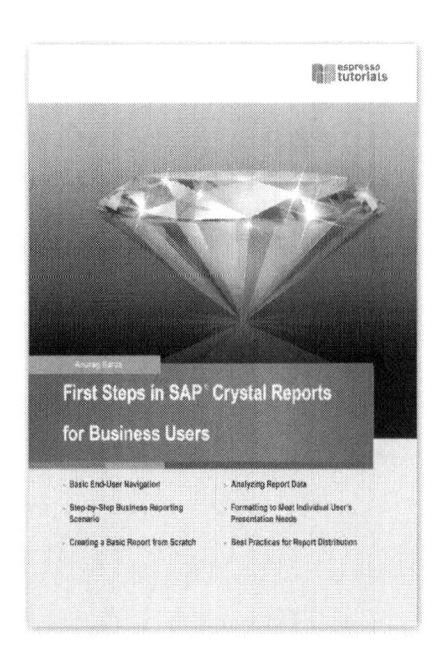

Anurag Barua
First Steps in SAP® Crystal Reports for Business Users

When SAP acquired Business Objects in 2008 Crystal Reports became a standard part of SAP's software and menu of reporting tools. This book written specifically for business users provides an introduction to SAP Crystal Reports using a real-world business reporting scenario and will enable you to create your first report.

We'll cover:

- ▶ Overview, history and evolution of Crystal Reports
- ▶ Basic end-user navigation
- ▶ Creating a basic report from scratch

- ▶ Formatting to meet individual user's presentation needs
- ▶ Analysis techniques such as using formulas, sorting/filtering, grouping, summarizing, and creating alerts
- ▶ Best practices for report distribution

Detailed screenshots and explanations paired with a business reporting scenario will prepare you step by step to work efficiently with SAP Crystal Report version 2011.

Printed in Great Britain
by Amazon